Two Full Length Prac
for the CogAT® – Form 7

First Edition

For Level 8 (Grade 2)

Written and Published by:
Top Grader LLC., USA
Learning That Delivers Results

Key Features:
- ✓ **2 full-length** practice tests
- ✓ All questions in **full color** that emulate the format of real CogAT®
- ✓ **Sample questions** with explanations at the start of each section
- ✓ **Answer key** for each section
- ✓ **Bonus!** – Get a **Free CogAT® tutoring lesson worth $18.99** at Top-Grader.com (instructions on page #197)

Printed in the United States of America.

CogAT® and Cognitive Abilities Test™ are the registered trademarks of Houghton Mifflin Harcourt Company that neither endorses nor sponsors this product.
ISBN: 0692732144
ISBN-13: 978-0692732144

INTRODUCTION

Dear Reader,

Top Grader has been coaching children on the gifted and talented tests for more than three years. When we got requests from parents to coach their children on the CogAT®, we went looking around for practice material on this test. While we started with what was 'available' in the market, we quickly realized that we could give these children a much better preparation if we developed quality content on our own.

So our academicians got on the job. After reviewing a lot of study material on CogAT® available both online and in print, we found that there is a void when it comes to high-quality, structured, and relevant content for the CogAT® test. This book is an attempt to fill that void; every question in this book has been carefully developed to provide children with the most appropriate content for practice. What's even better is that all the questions in this book are in **'full-color'**, something that is essential to simulate the real CogAT® **test experience** but is hard to find in the current marketplace.

Although we cannot guarantee that the content of this book will help every child ace the CogAT®, we do assure you, based on our experience coaching prospective CogAT® test takers, that if a child solved all the problems available in the two practice tests in this book, his or her chances of getting a high score will improve greatly.

If you feel your child needs personal attention and hand-holding to prepare for the CogAT®, we encourage you to take advantage of our one-on-one online tutoring for the CogAT® test at www.top-grader.com. To make it easy for you, we are offering a **free lesson worth US $18.99**. Please follow the instructions on page #197 to register your interest.

The Top Grader team wishes you and/or your child 'best of luck' for the CogAT® test! We value your feedback to help us improve our products and services, hence if you have any questions, comments, or suggestions, please do not hesitate to reach out to us at feedback@top-grader.com.

Warmest Regards,

Top Grader Team

TABLE OF CONTENTS

ALL YOU NEED TO KNOW ABOUT THE COGAT®

The CogAT® or the Cognitive Abilities Test™ is a form of gifted and talented assessment to identify academically gifted children. It measures a child's cognitive abilities that are developed or acquired over a period of time through experiential learning both in and out of school. The Cognitive Abilities Test™ (CogAT®) Form 7 reflects the most current industry research in the measurement of cognitive abilities and learning styles.

How is CogAT® Form 7 different?
CogAT® Form 7 differs from earlier editions of the test, in that it makes the assessment more accessible to ELL (English Language Learner) children for three reasons. First, only one of the three tests on the Verbal Battery (Sentence Completion) and none of the items on the three Quantitative tests require comprehension of oral language—resulting in a more meaningful assessment of every student's reasoning ability. Second, items used on the new primary-level tests were selected from a larger pool of items specifically designed to be fair to ELL children. Finally, the total testing time is slightly less compared to previous editions.

What is the use of CogAT®?
The test is primarily used to assess a child's reasoning abilities that are linked to academic success. When administered with The Iowa Tests, the CogAT® can also provide predicted achievement scores. The data gathered from the tests inform instructional practices that best meet the needs of each student and expand educational opportunities for all students. Educators can use the Ability Profile Score to make important decisions about placing students in different learning programs such as the Extended Learning Programs and the Gifted and Talented Programs in school.

What are the editions of CogAT®?
The CogAT® comes in two editions – the **primary edition** and the **multilevel edition**. The primary edition of form 7 is designed for children in kindergarten through grade 2 (Levels 5/6, 7, 8) while the multilevel edition is designed for children in grades 3 through 12 (Levels 9 to 17/18).

What is tested on each edition of the CogAT®?
The CogAT® measures a child's cognitive abilities in three sections - Verbal, Quantitative, and Non-Verbal. Each section consists of 3 subsets with different question formats. In the **primary edition (grades K to 2)**, no reading is required since all directions are read aloud by the teacher or the test administrator, who paces children through all the questions in the subsets. In the **multilevel edition (grades 3 to 12)**, the picture-based, teacher-paced verbal and quantitative sections of the primary edition transition to the text and numeric-based, timed verbal and quantitative sections.

To find the key differences between primary and multilevel edition and between the subsets in each, please refer the table on the next page:

CogAT® Form 7	Primary Edition (K to 2) All directions read aloud by the teacher/administrator and the batteries are teacher-paced	Multilevel Edition (3 to 12) All directions are read by the child himself and the batteries are self-paced
Verbal Battery	Picture Analogies	Verbal Analogies
	Sentence Completion (teacher reads out the sentence in the question)	Sentence Completion
	Picture Classification	Verbal Classification
Quantitative Battery	Number Analogies	Number Analogies
	Number Puzzles	Number Puzzles
	Number Series	Number Series
Non-Verbal Battery	Figure Matrices	Figure Matrices
	Paper Folding	Paper Folding
	Figure Classification	Figure Classification

Directions on attempting the questions in each subset are provided before the start of each subset in this book.

How many questions are there in each subset of the CogAT®?

The number of questions in each subset differ for each level of the CogAT®. Each subset has either one or two sample questions to begin with. Refer the below table for details:

CogAT® Form 7	Session	Subset	Number of Questions				
			Level 5/6	Level 7	Level 8	Level 9	Level 10-17/18
Verbal Battery	1	Sample Items	2	2	2	2	2
		Picture/Verbal Analogies	14	16	18	22	24
	2	Sample Items	1	1	1	1	2
		Sentence Completion	14	16	18	20	20
	3	Sample Items	2	2	2	2	2
		Picture/Verbal Classification	14	16	18	20	20
Quantitative Battery	4	Sample Items	2	2	2	2	2
		Number Analogies	14	16	18	18	18
	5	Sample Items	2	2	2	2	2
		Number Puzzles	10	12	14	16	16
	6	Sample Items	2	2	2	2	2
		Number Series	14	16	18	18	18
Non-Verbal Battery	7	Sample Items	2	2	2	2	2
		Figure Matrices	14	16	18	20	22
	8	Sample Items	2	2	2	2	2
		Paper Folding	10	12	14	16	16
	9	Sample Items	2	2	2	2	2
		Figure Classification	14	16	18	20	22

TEST TAKING TIPS: **THE RULE OF FOUR**

Here are our **four rules** that you should use for every question on the CogAT® test:

1. **First, solve the question in your head**
   Before you even look at the answer options, try solving the question in your head and visualizing the answer. You will be surprised to know that more often than not, you would already know what the correct answer looks like.

2. **Second, look at all the answer options**
   After you have figured out the correct answer in your head, look at all the answer options. Although you would think you know the correct answer, sometimes looking at answer options will help you avoid a trap that test developers set for you. These traps are 'illusions' that resemble the answer in your head but are not exactly the same, so pay close attention to avoid selecting the wrong option.

3. **Third, eliminate the wrong options**
   This is a very important strategy. When you look at all the answer options, you will find atleast one or two options that don't even come close to the answer you are looking for. By eliminating these options from your consideration, you are improving your chances of selecting the correct answer. It is easier to figure the correct answer when you have to choose from two rather than four answer options, right?

4. **Fourth, guess intelligently and move on**
   Ultimately, your aim is to get as many correct answers as possible on the CogAT® questions. Since there is no negative marking for incorrect answers on the test, if you can't figure out the correct answer after using rules 1, 2, and 3, it is better that you guess than leave the question blank. However, always guess between the options that remain after applying rule 3 as that will increase your chances of guessing right!

Before The Test

Give yourself enough time to prepare
An ideal CogAT® preparation calls for a well-paced study plan spread across 2-3 months of time ahead of your test day. You need to practice and review multiple times to become better at solving CogAT® type of questions.

Practice, Practice, Practice!
Everyone knows this - Practice will help you get better! Keep practicing with as many questions as you can. And while you practice, do not forget to review your answers against each question. It is always a good practice to mark the questions that you got wrong in your first attempt and revisit them 2-3 times to master them completely.

Eat well and rest well
Do not get so bogged down by the test syndrome that you ignore eating and resting. Eat all your meals, especially a healthy breakfast every day to keep you going. Sleep atleast 7-8 hours a day as that is the minimum amount of sleep you need daily to keep your brain's performance at the optimum level.

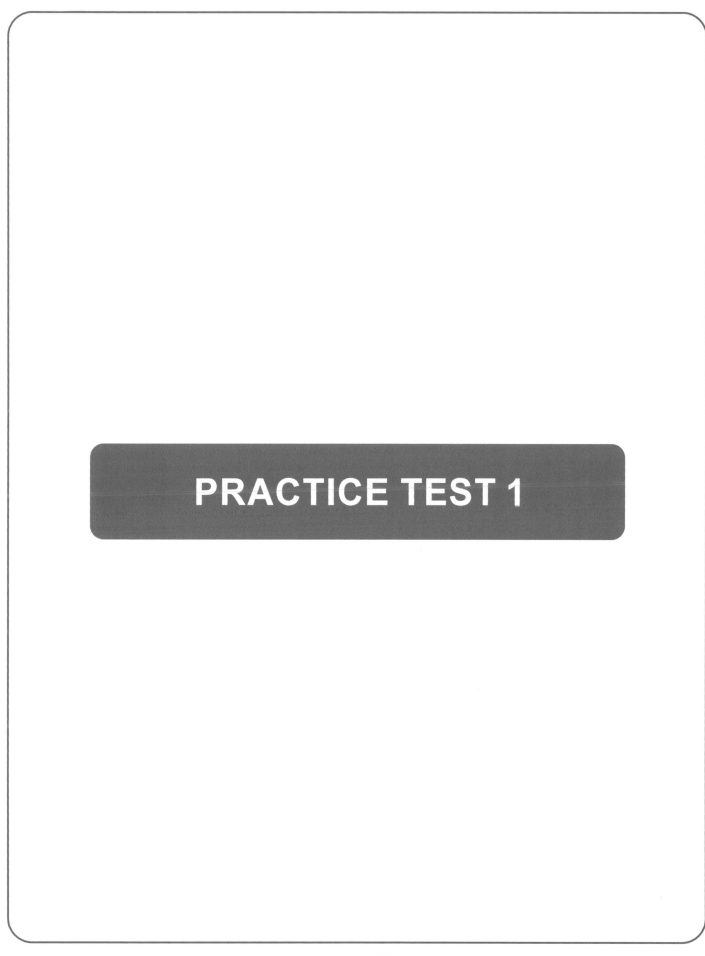

PRACTICE TEST 1

Subset 1: Picture Analogies

Instructions:

For each of the questions in this subset, you have to first determine the relationship between the two pictures in the top row. Next, look at the first picture in the bottom row and from the options provided to you, find the picture that best completes the relationship in the same way as the relationship between the two pictures in the top row. Color the bubble under one option (A,B, or C) that is the best match.

The first two questions are samples and have been solved for you.

1.

C is correct. Your aim is to find the option that best fits the empty box in the bottom row shown by "?". The two pictures in the top row show a relationship between a key and a door. The key opens the door. The first picture in the bottom row is a key and is supposed to be related in the same way (as the pictures in top row) to one of the pictures in options A, B, and C. Option A is incorrect because a key can't open a number coded lock. Answer B is also incorrect because a key can't open a sword! The key looks like a key to a car or a vehicle, which is option C.

2.

A is correct. Your aim is to find the option that best fits the empty box in the bottom row shown by "?". The two pictures in the top row show a relationship between a golf ball and a golf club. The golf ball is played with a golf club. The first picture in the bottom row is a tennis ball and is supposed to be related in the same way (as the pictures in top row) to one of the pictures in options A, B, and C. Option B is incorrect because a ball can't be played with a camera! Answer C is also incorrect because a tennis ball can't be played with a basketball net! The tennis ball can be played with a tennis racket, which is option A.

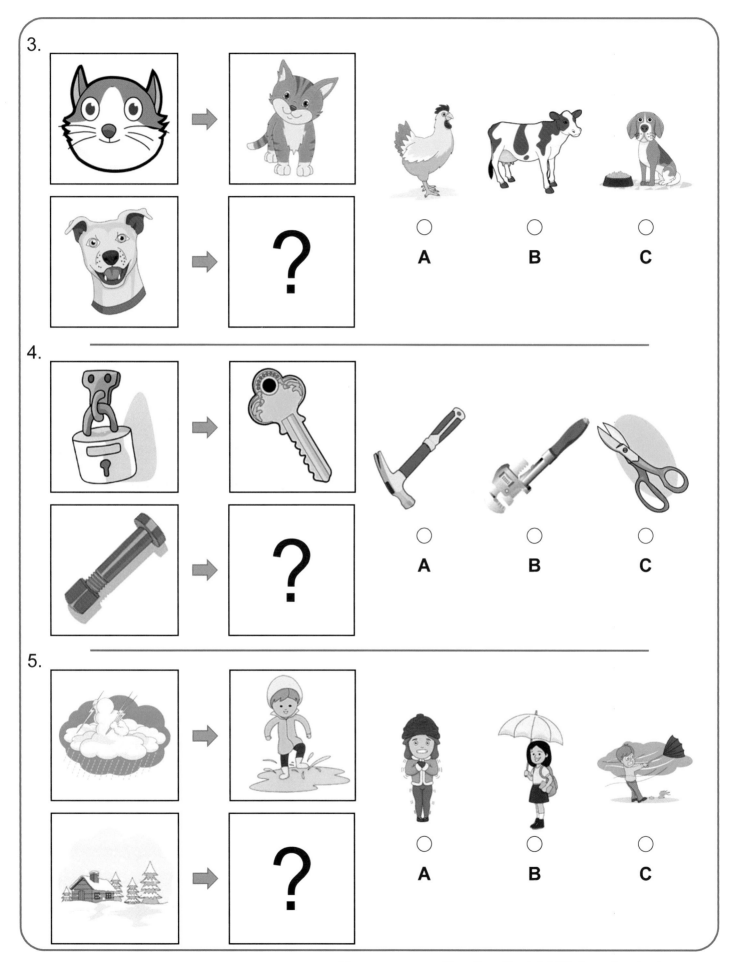

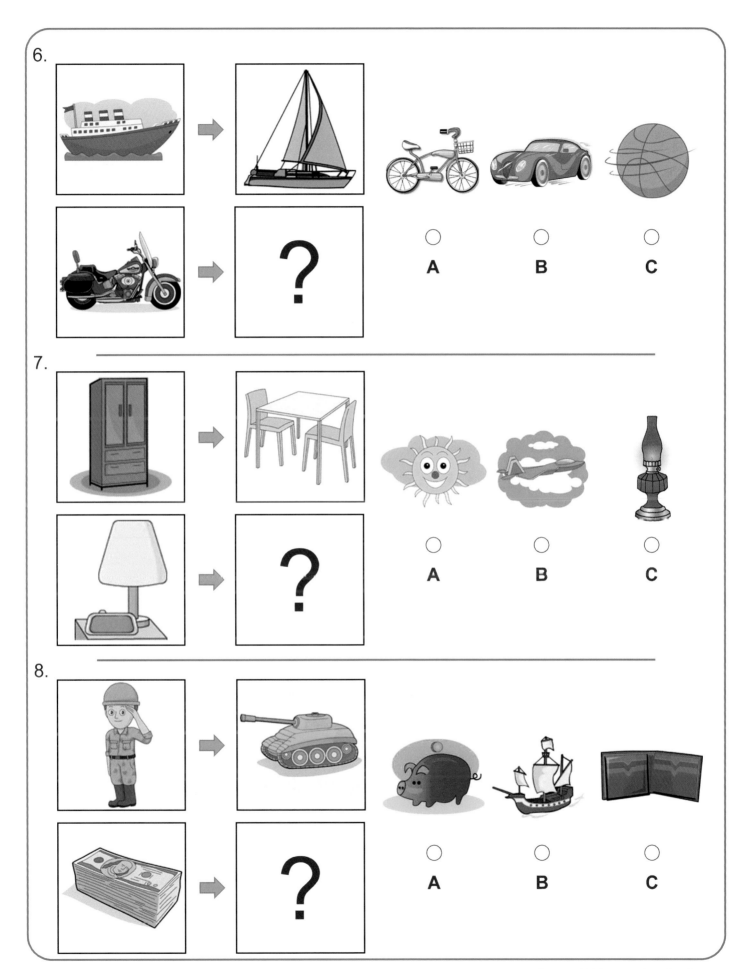

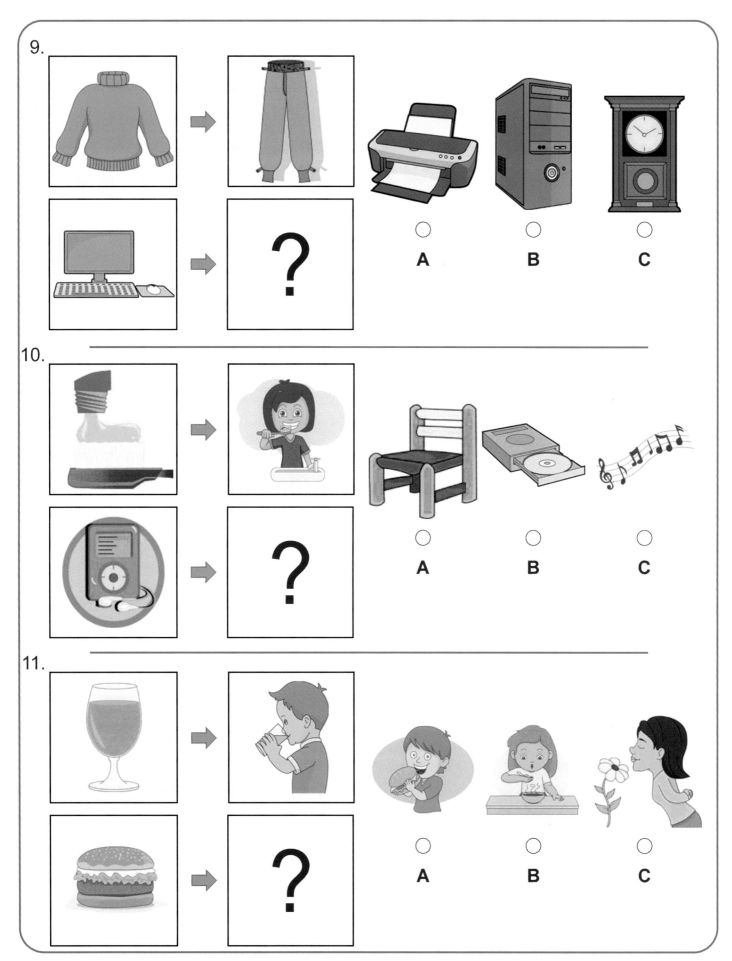

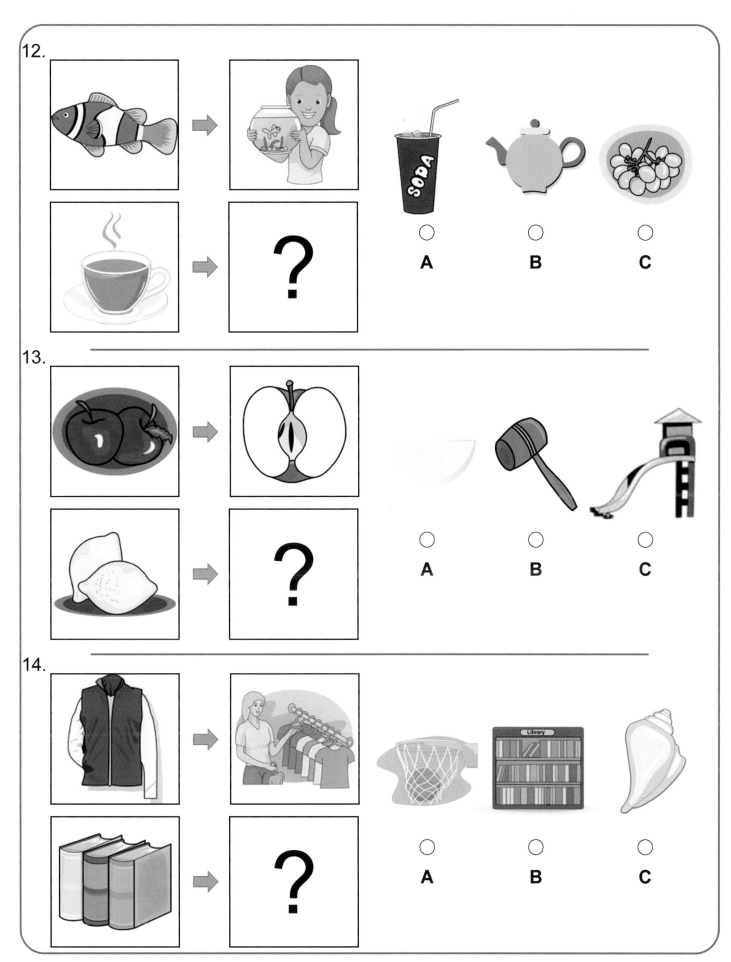

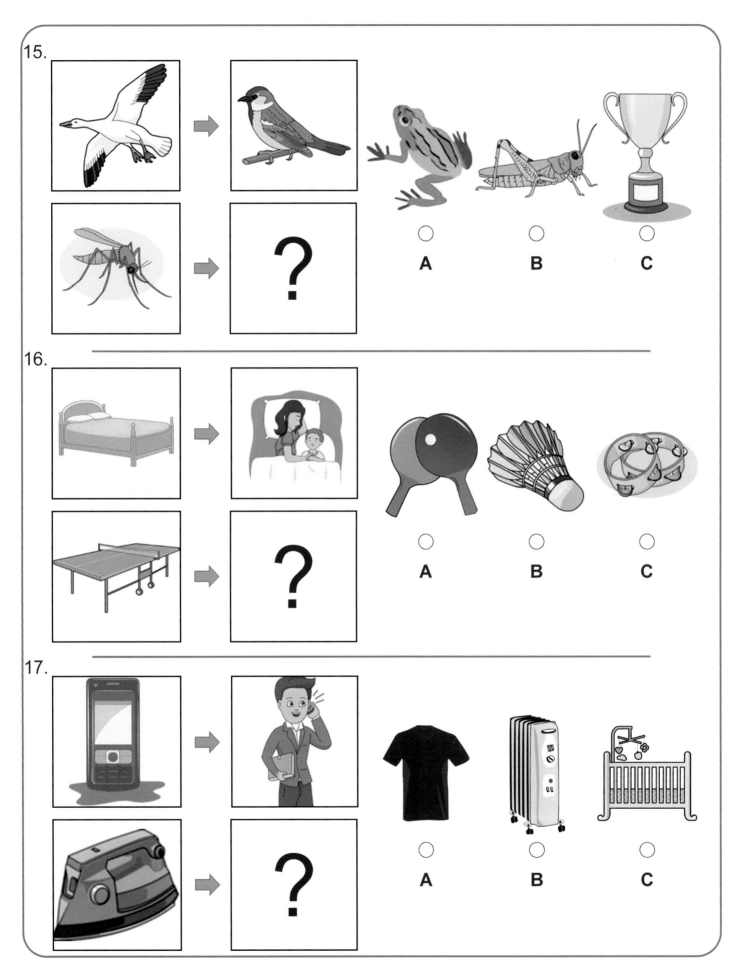

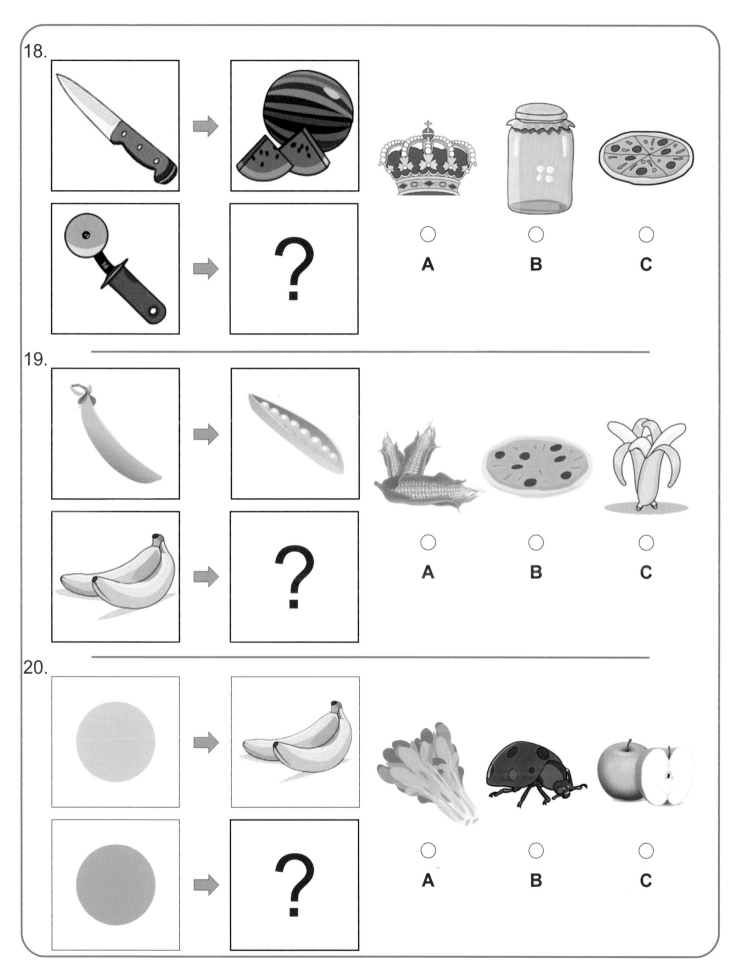

Subset 2: Sentence Completion

Instructions:

In the primary edition (grades K to 2 / levels 5/6 to 8), the questions in this subset will be read out to you by the teacher or the administrator. Listen to what is read out very carefully as some of the sentences may have a 'not', 'non' or 'un-' words that reverse the meaning of the sentence.

For each of the questions in this subset, find the picture that best answers the sentence in the question. Color the bubble under one option (A,B, or C) that is the best match.

The first question is a sample and has been solved for you.

1. Which one of these is most likely used for hair?

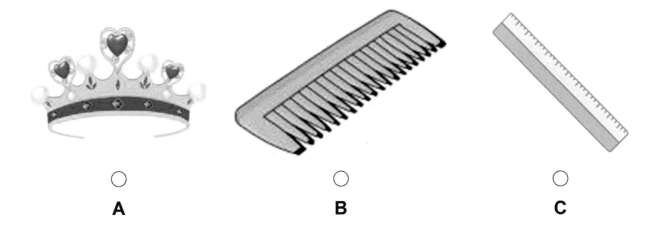

A   B   C

B is correct. A is incorrect because a crown is normally an ornament worn on the head as a symbol of achievement. C is also incorrect because it is a ruler used to measure length of objects. B is a comb that is used to arrange and groom hair, the only correct option.

2. Eva has to take a bath before she goes to school. Which one of these pictures shows what Eva has to do?

A   B   C

3. This kitten is playful and loves to play with the ball. Which one of these shows what the kitten loves to do?

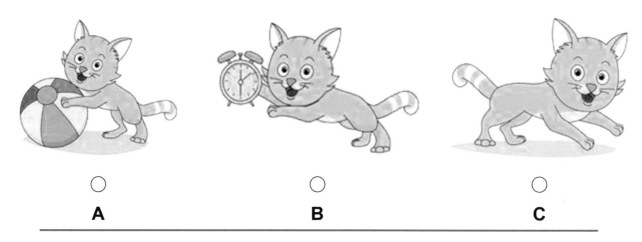

A   B   C

4. Where does the dog rest?

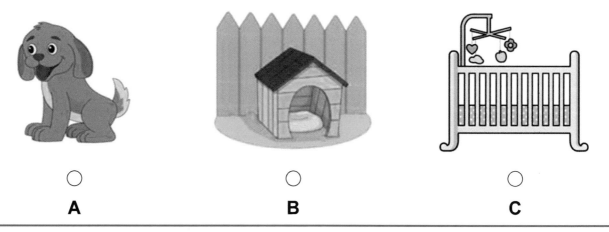

A   B   C

5. Which one of these is the tallest animal?

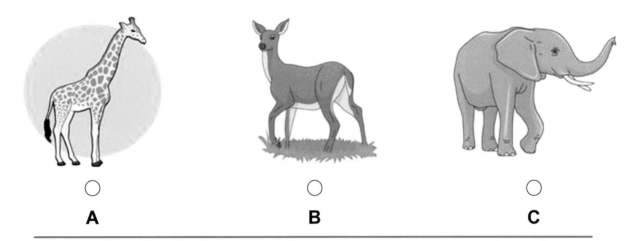

A   B   C

6. Which one of these animals likes to eats grass?

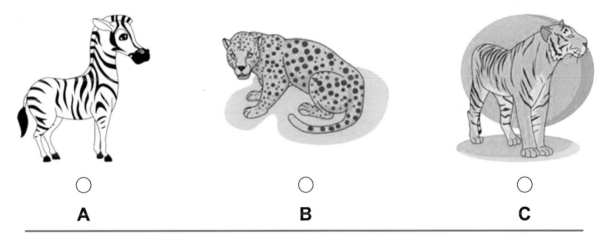

A   B   C

7. Which one of these building is the smallest in size?

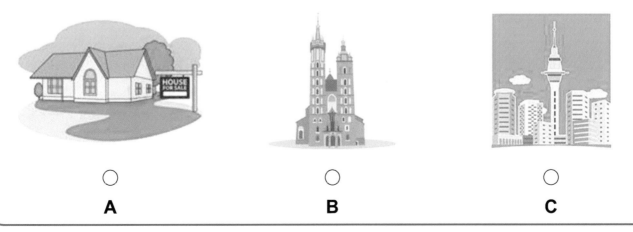

A   B   C

8. Which one of these is most likely to be found in library?

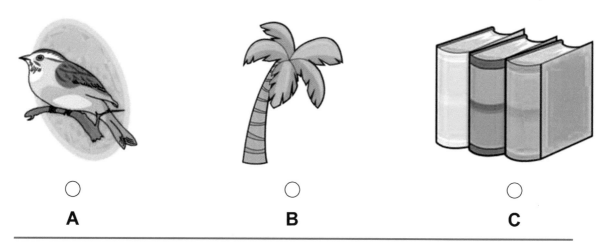

A   B   C

9. Mary asked John to cut the paper into half. Which one of these is John most likely to use to follow Mary's instruction?

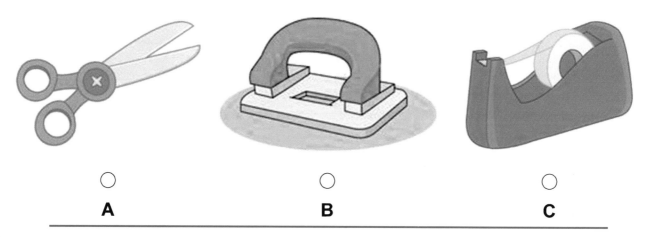

A   B   C

10. "All posters must be pasted on the wall by 9 AM tomorrow", said the teacher to Alex. Which one of these is Alex most likely to use to follow the teacher's order?

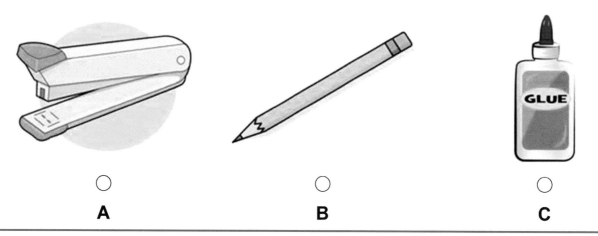

A   B   C

11. Which one of these is "hot" drink?

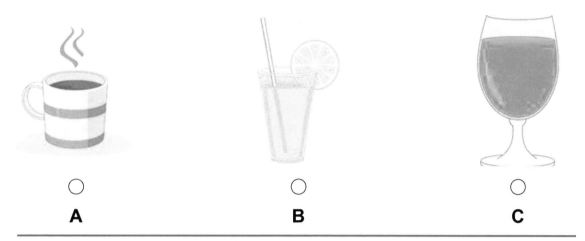

| A | B | C |

12. Which one of these would you use to paint a wall?

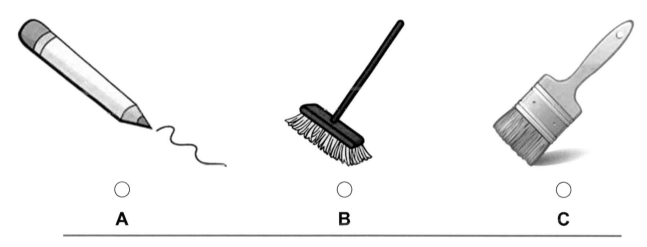

| A | B | C |

13. Which one of these birds gives us eggs?

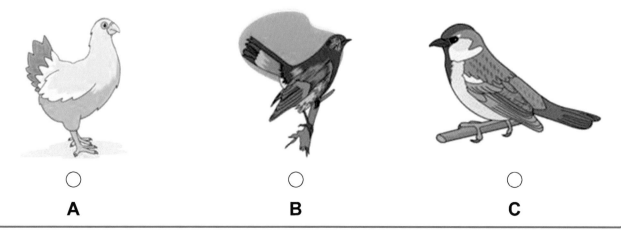

| A | B | C |

14. Sam is going for deep sea diving activity. Which one of these would he be needing most during this activity?

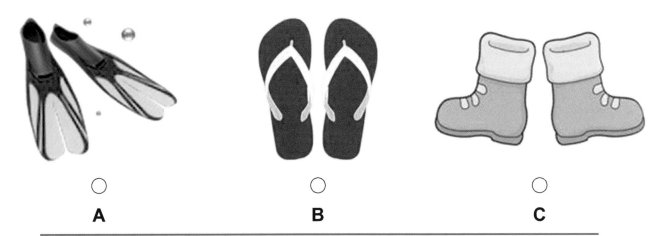

A

B

C

15. Which one of these is a part of a body of an animal?

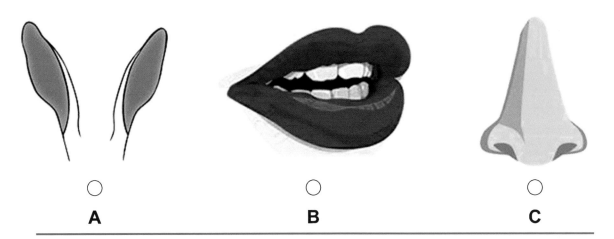

A

B

C

16. Where does an Eskimo live?

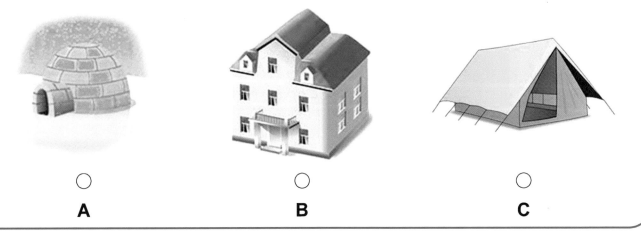

A

B

C

17. Which one of these is used to click a photograph?

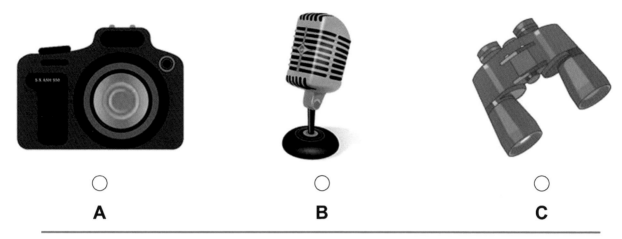

A   B   C

18. Which one of these is edible?

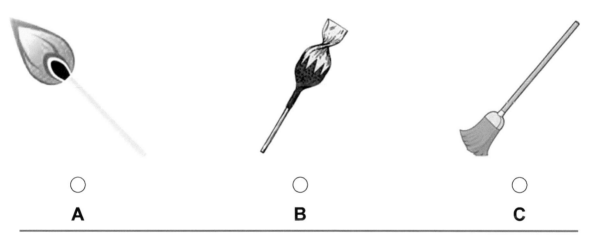

A   B   C

19. As she is sick, Samantha has been advised by the doctor to be on a hygienic and liquid only diet. Which one of these will Samantha not use for her diet during her sickness?

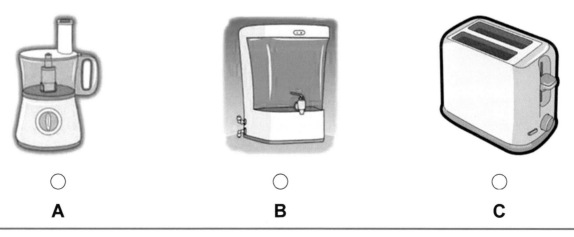

A   B   C

Subset 3: Picture Classification

Instructions:

For each of the questions in this subset, first look at the three pictures above the line and determine how they are similar as objects or activities. Next, look at the pictures below the line and color the bubble under one option (A,B, or C) that is the best match.

The first two questions are samples and have been solved for you.

1.

A   B   C

C is correct. The three pictures in the top row are of animals that belong to the cat family. A is incorrect because it is a dog. B is incorrect because it is a cow. C is a house cat that belongs to the cat family, the only correct option.

2.

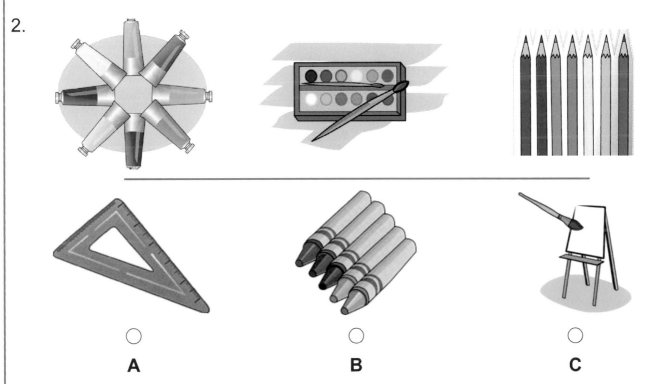

A   B   C

B is correct. The three pictures in the top row are of coloring objects. A is incorrect because it is an instrument used for geometrical drawings. C is incorrect because it is a canvas. B is a bunch of crayons used for coloring, the only correct option.

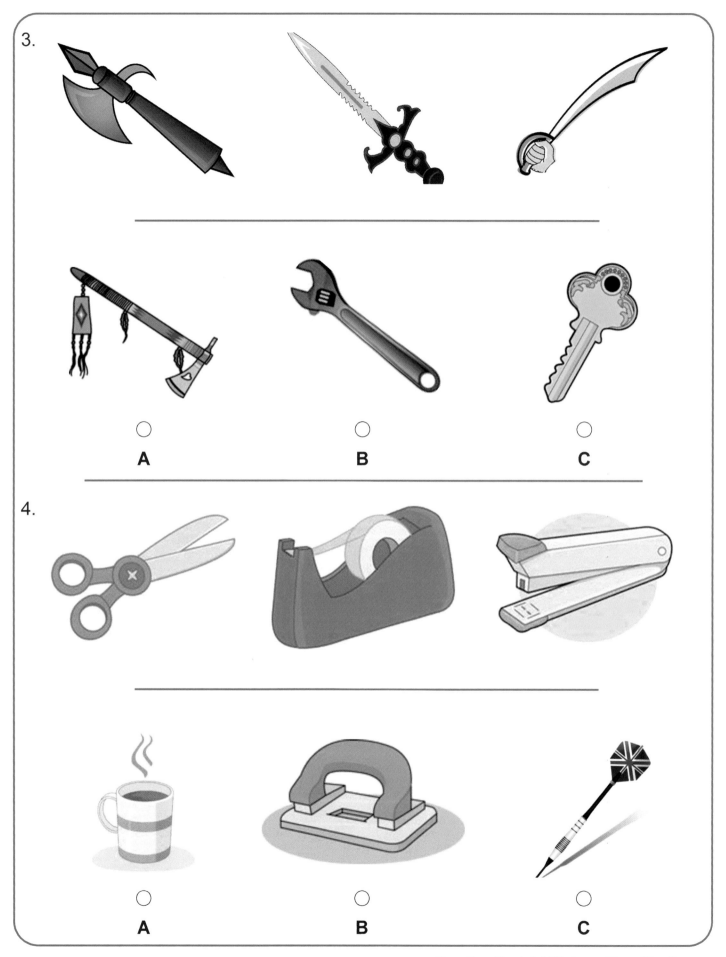

3.

A ○

B ○

C ○

4.

A ○

B ○

C ○

5.

A

B

C

6.

A

B

C

9.

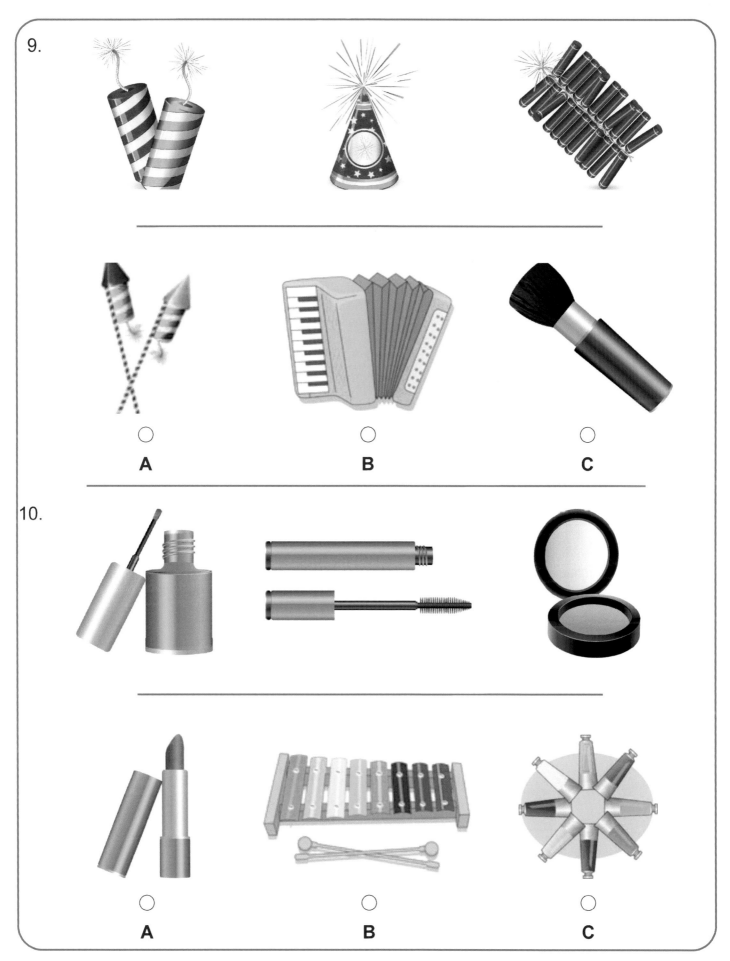

A ○

B ○

C ○

10.

A ○

B ○

C ○

11.

○ A ○ B ○ C

12.

○ A ○ B ○ C

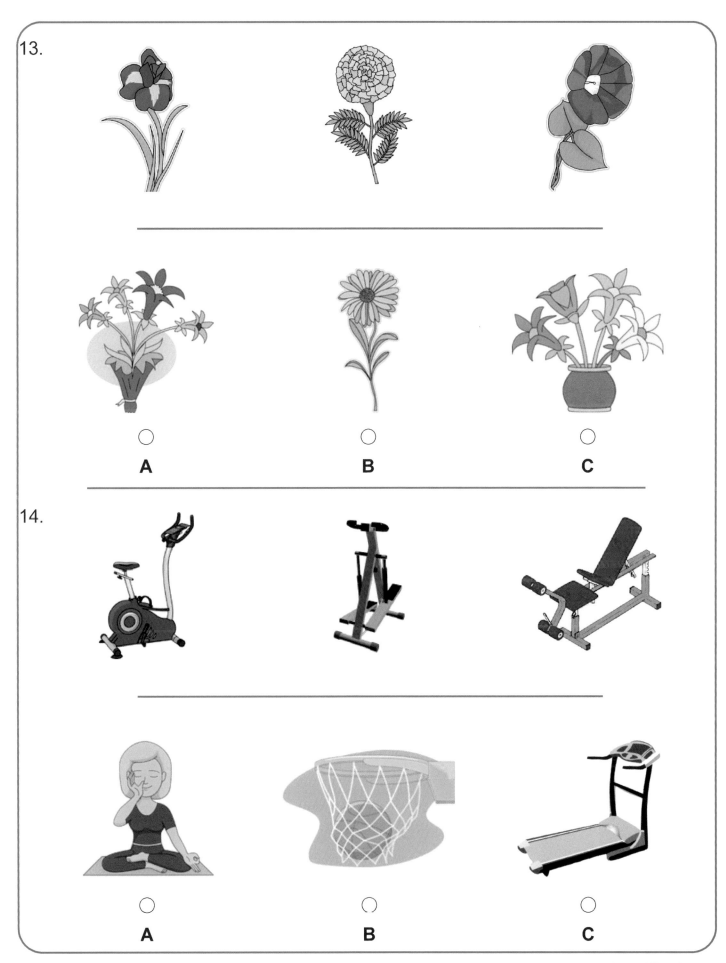

15.

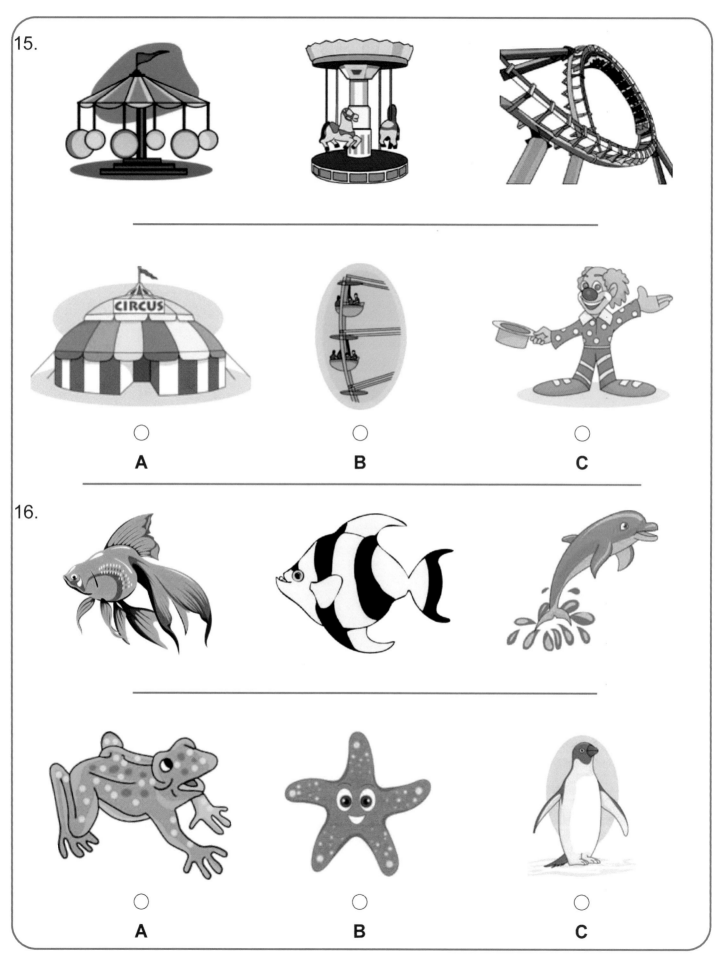

A   B   C

16.

A   B   C

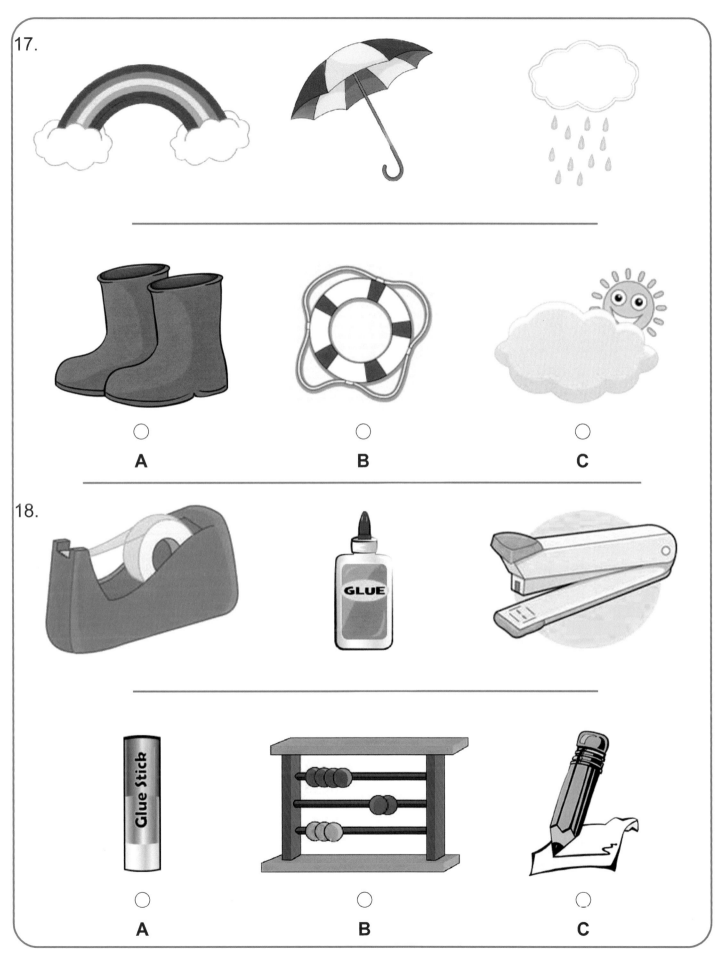

17.

A   B   C

18.

A   B   C

19.

A

B

C

20.

A

B

C

Subset 4: Number Analogies

Instructions:

For each of the questions in this subset, you have to first determine the relationship between the number of objects shown in two pictures in the top row. Next, look at the first picture in the bottom row and from the options provided to you, find the picture that best completes the relationship in the same way as the relationship between the two pictures in the top row. Color the bubble under one option (A,B, or C) that is the best match.

The first two questions are samples and have been solved for you.

1.

C is correct. In the top row, the first picture shows 6 pencils while the second picture shows 3 pencils, half the number of pencils in the first picture (1/2 X 6 = 3). In the bottom row, the first picture is that of 4 pens. We need to look for an option which shows half of 4 pens which is equal to 2 pens (1/2 X 4 = 2). Only C shows 2 pens and is the correct option.

2.

B is correct. In the top row, the first picture shows 1 table with 4 legs and 1 chair with 4 legs while the second picture shows the sum total of legs of the table and chair (4 + 4 = 8). In the bottom row, the first picture shows 1 table and 2 chairs. We need to look for an option which shows the sum total of the legs of the table and 2 chairs shown in first picture (4 + 4 + 4 = 12). Only B shows 12 legs and is the correct option.

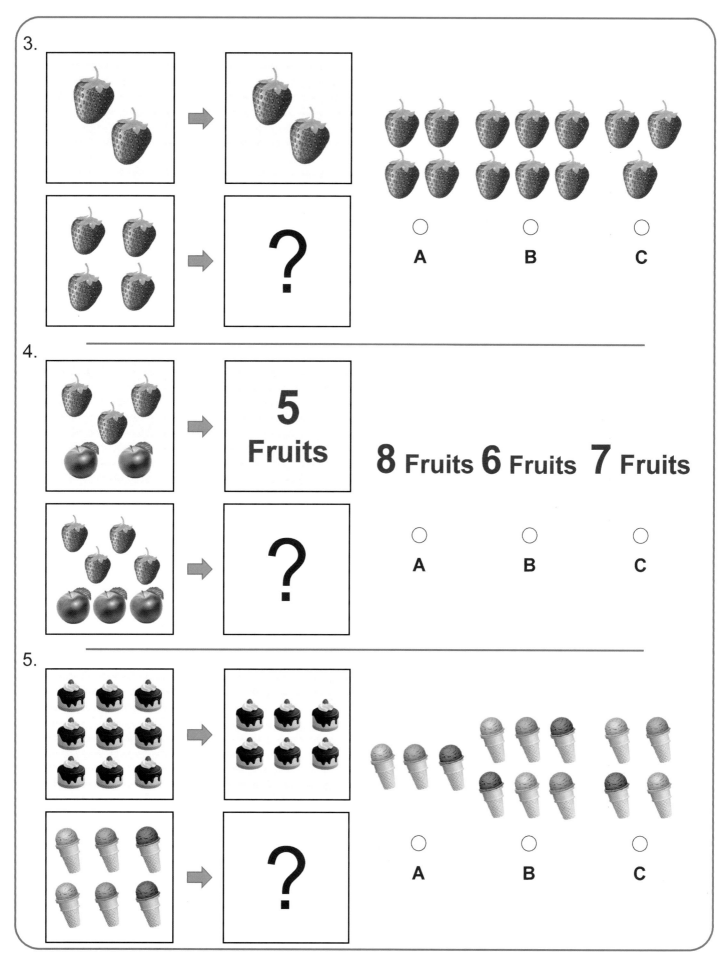

3.

4.

5 Fruits

8 Fruits 6 Fruits 7 Fruits

5.

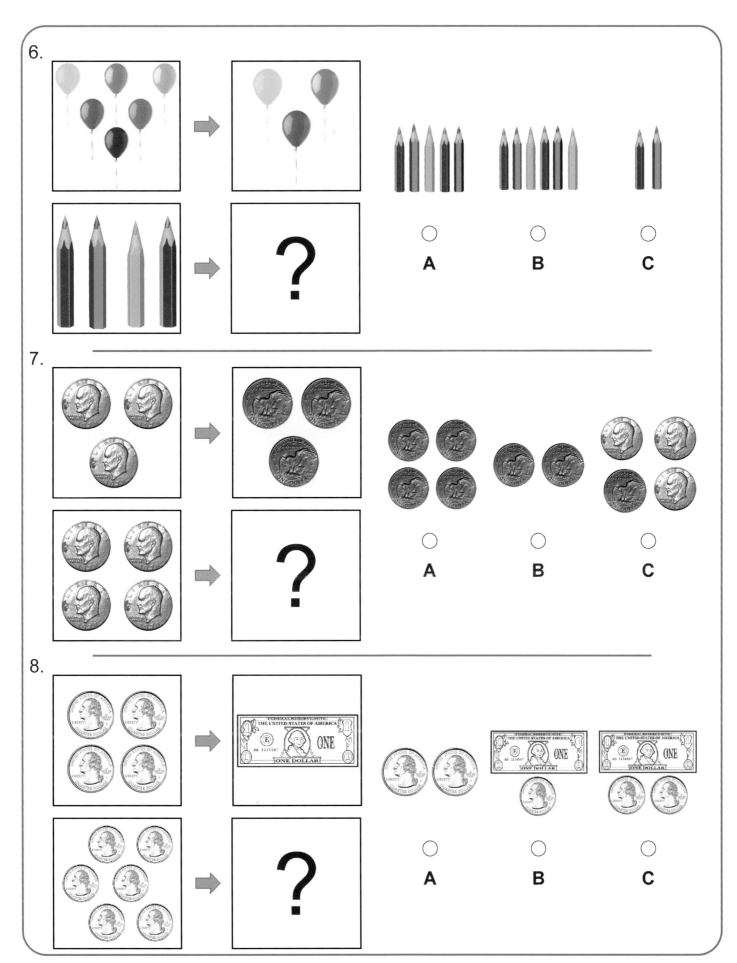

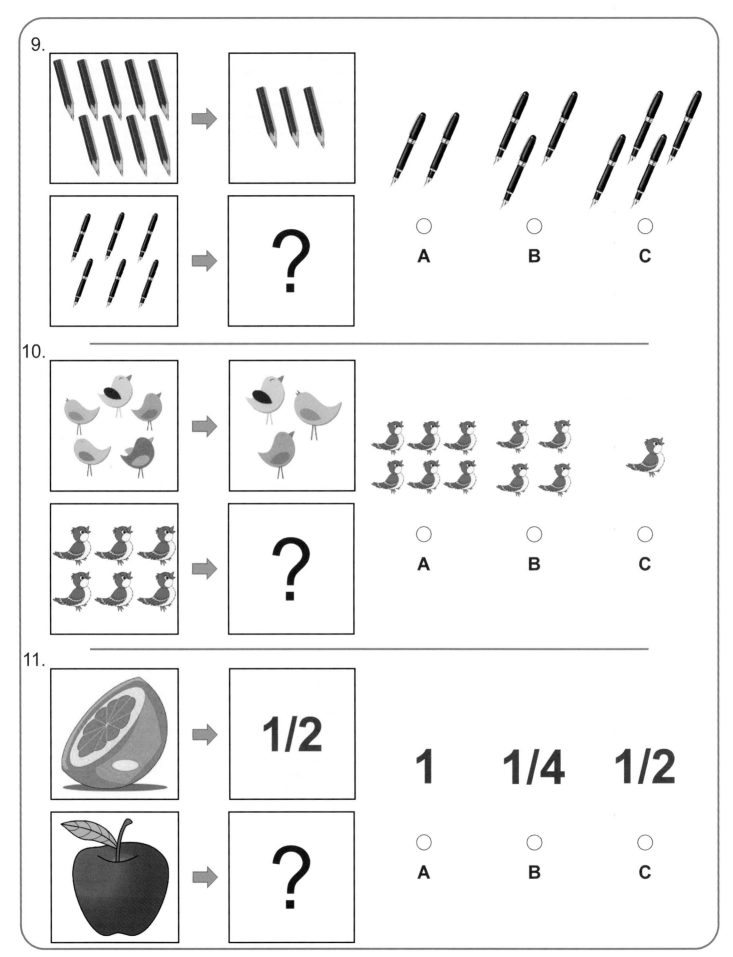

9.

10.

11.

1   1/4   1/2

A   B   C

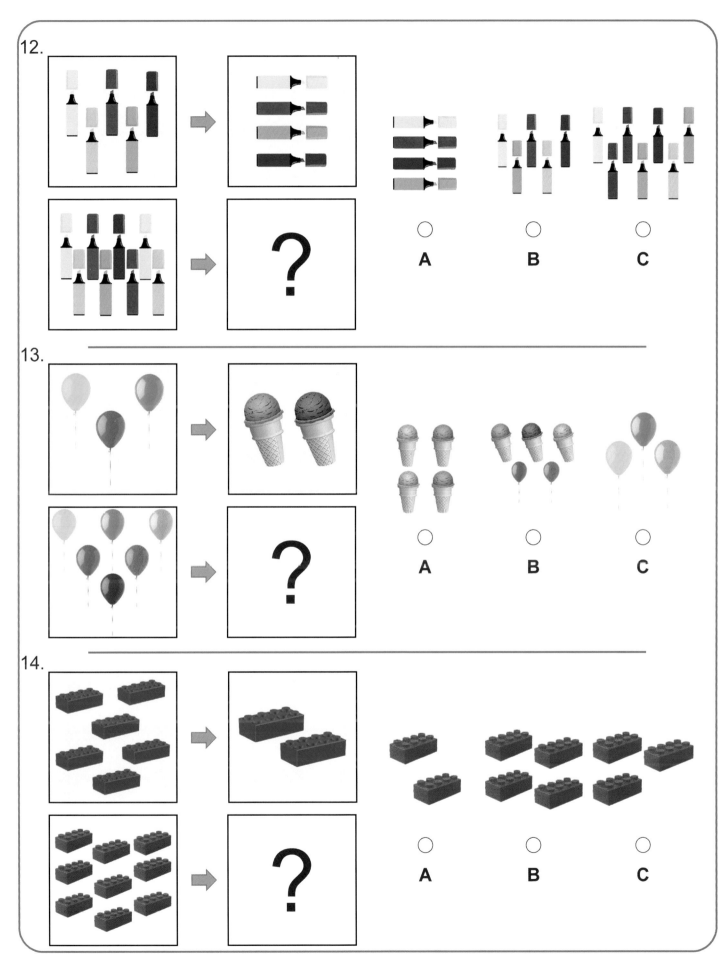

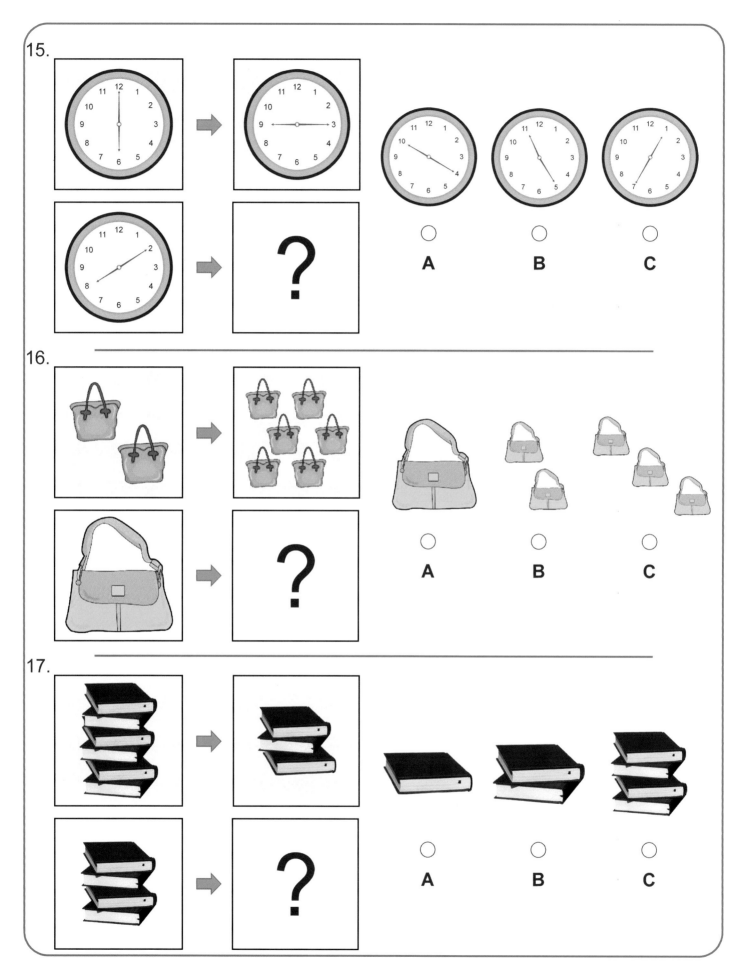

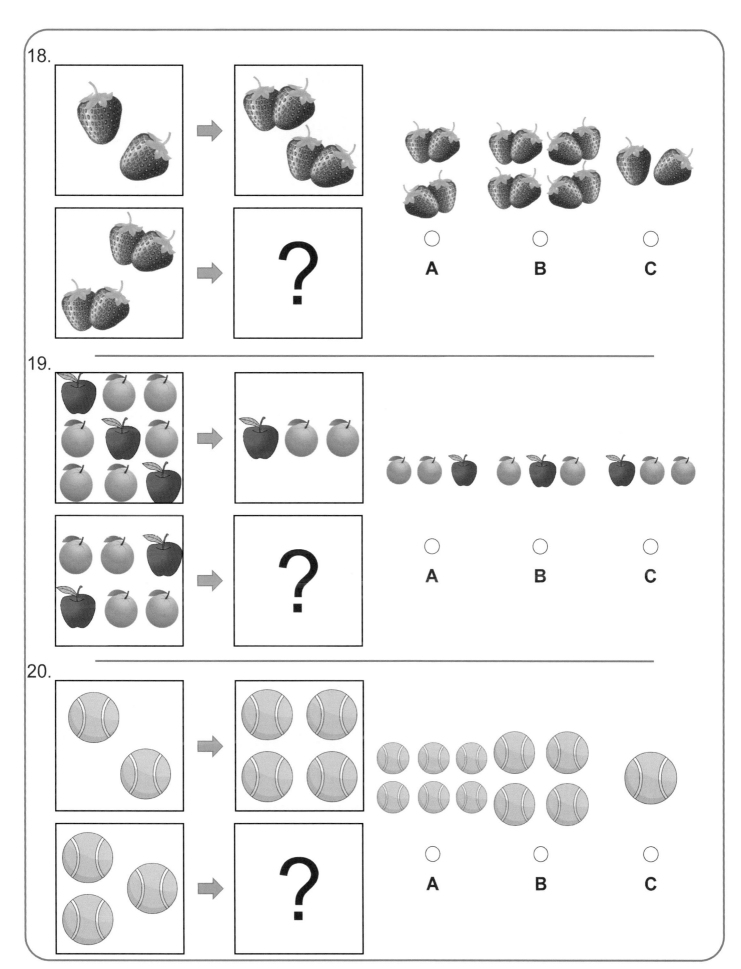

Subset 5: Number Puzzles

Instructions:

For each of the questions in this subset, you will see two trains on either side of the line with cars attached to them. The number of cars attached to each of these trains may not always be the same or there may be no cars attached at all. The cars in each of these trains carry different load.

From the answer options provided to you, you need to find the car that when replaced with the empty car in the question (shown by a "?") balances the load in both the trains. Color the bubble under one option (A,B, or C) that is the best match.

The first two questions are samples and have been solved for you.

1.

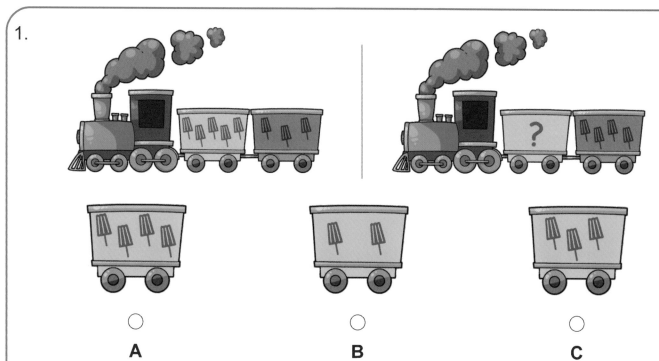

○	○	○
A	**B**	**C**

A is correct. Your job is to make sure that the trains on either side carry the same load. The picture of the train on the left shows there are 5 ice cream bars in the green car and 3 ice cream bars in the pink car. The total of the green and pink cars is 8 (5+3). Now look at the picture of the train on the right. It shows there are 4 ice cream bars in the pink car. You need 4 more ice cream bars in the green car to make the total equal to 8. Only A has 4 ice cream bars and is the correct answer.

2.

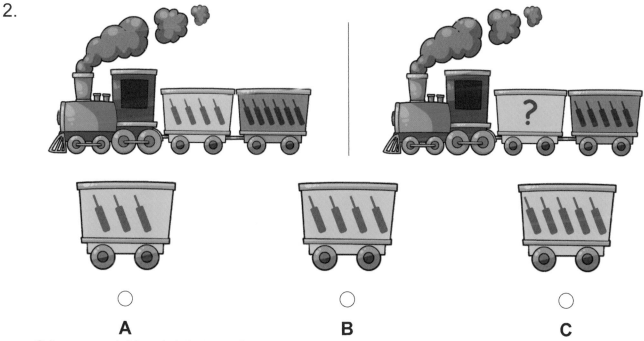

○	○	○
A	**B**	**C**

C is correct. Your job is to make sure that the trains on either side carry the same load. The picture of the train on the left shows there are 4 bats in the green car and 6 bats in the pink car. The total of the green and pink cars is 10 (4+6). Now look at the picture of the train on the right. It shows there are 5 bats in the pink car. You need 5 more bats in the green car to make the total equal to 10. Only C has 5 bats and is the correct answer.

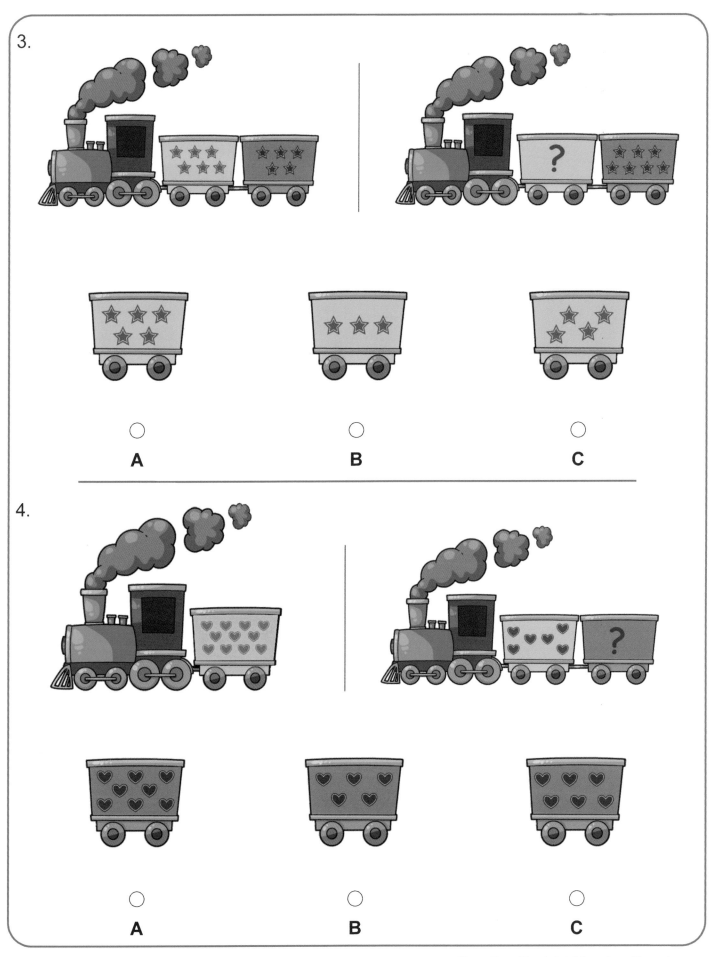

3.

A

B

C

4.

A

B

C

Practice Test 1 | Number Puzzles

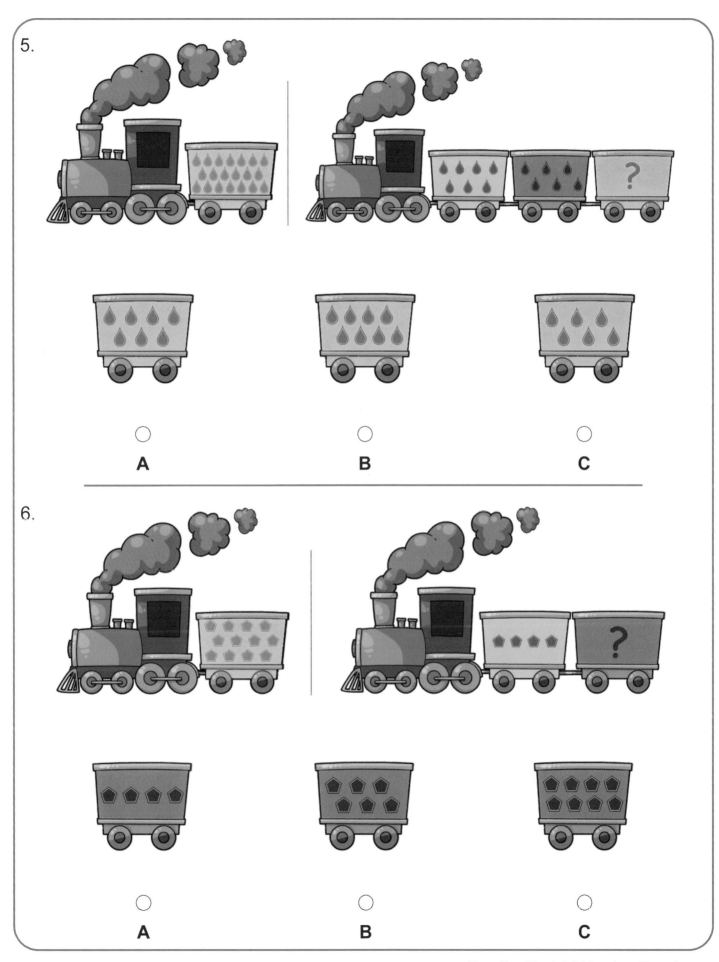

5.

A

B

C

6.

A

B

C

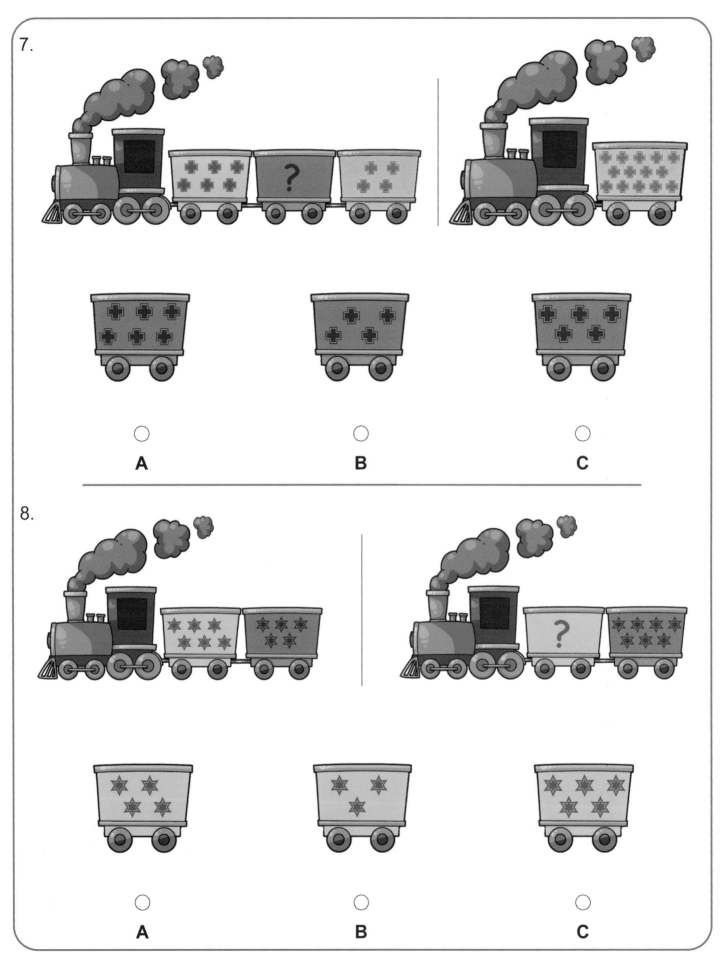

7.

A   B   C

8.

A   B   C

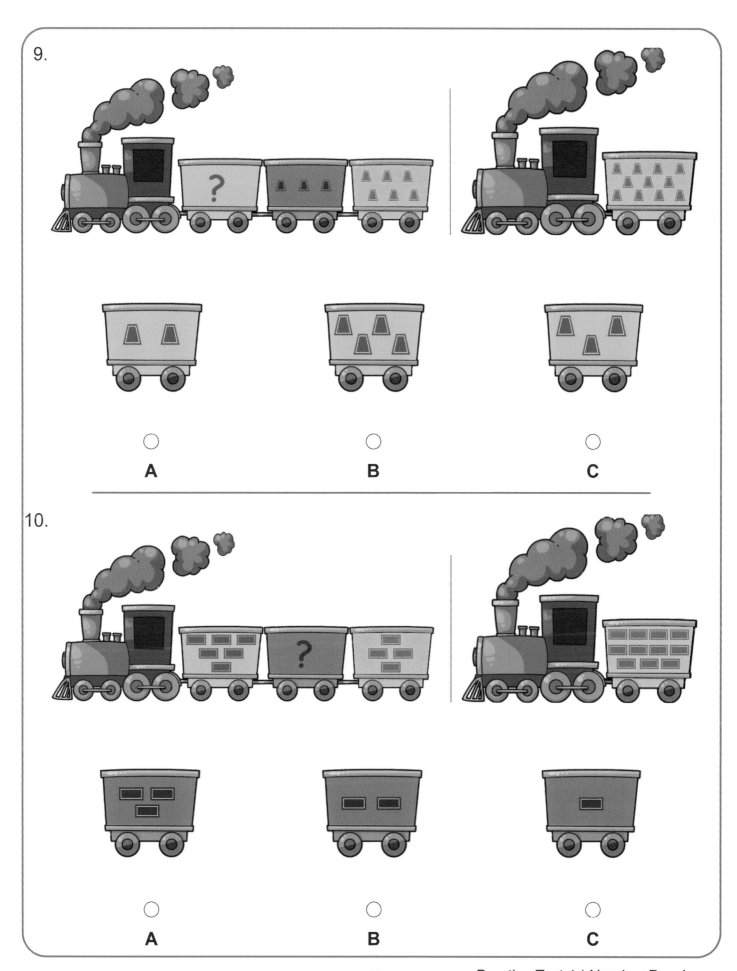

9.

A   B   C

10.

A   B   C

11.

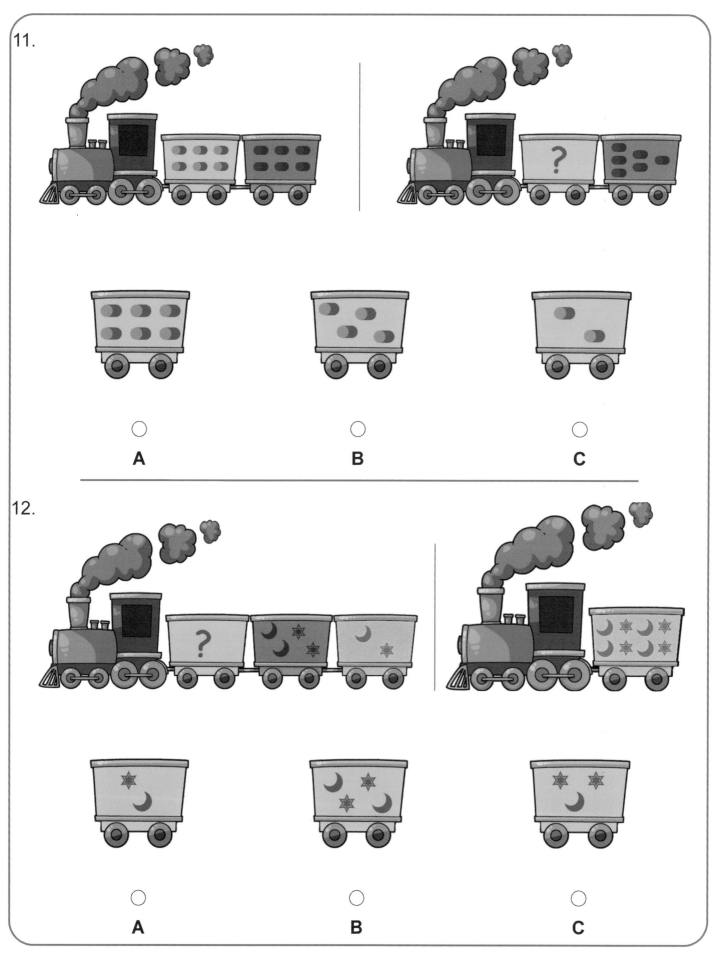

A

B

C

12.

A

B

C

Practice Test 1 | Number Puzzles

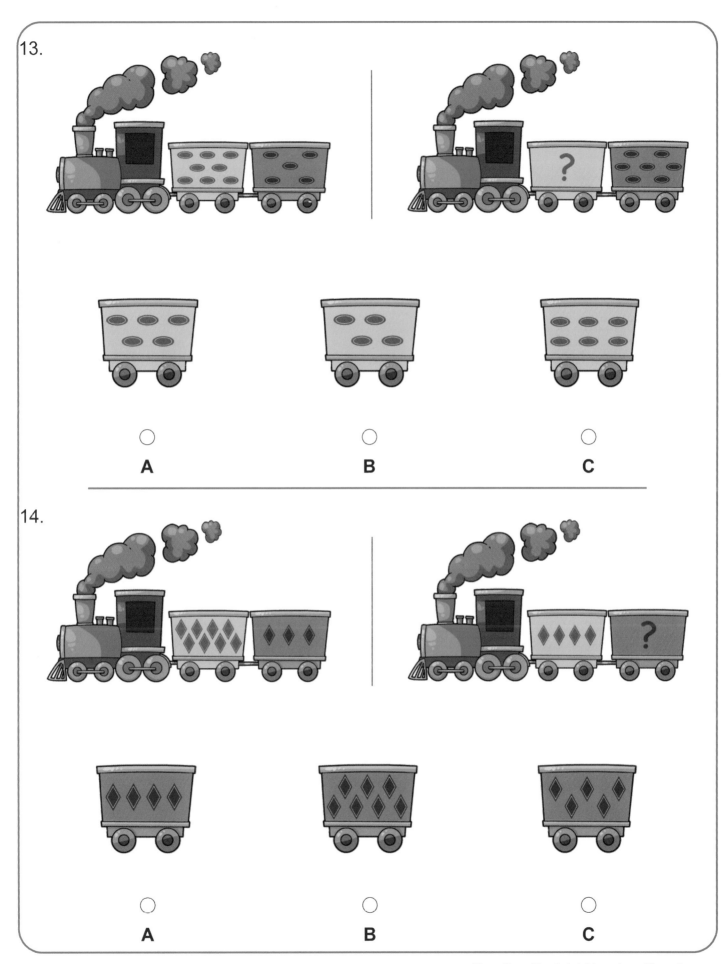

13.

A   B   C

14.

A   B   C

15.

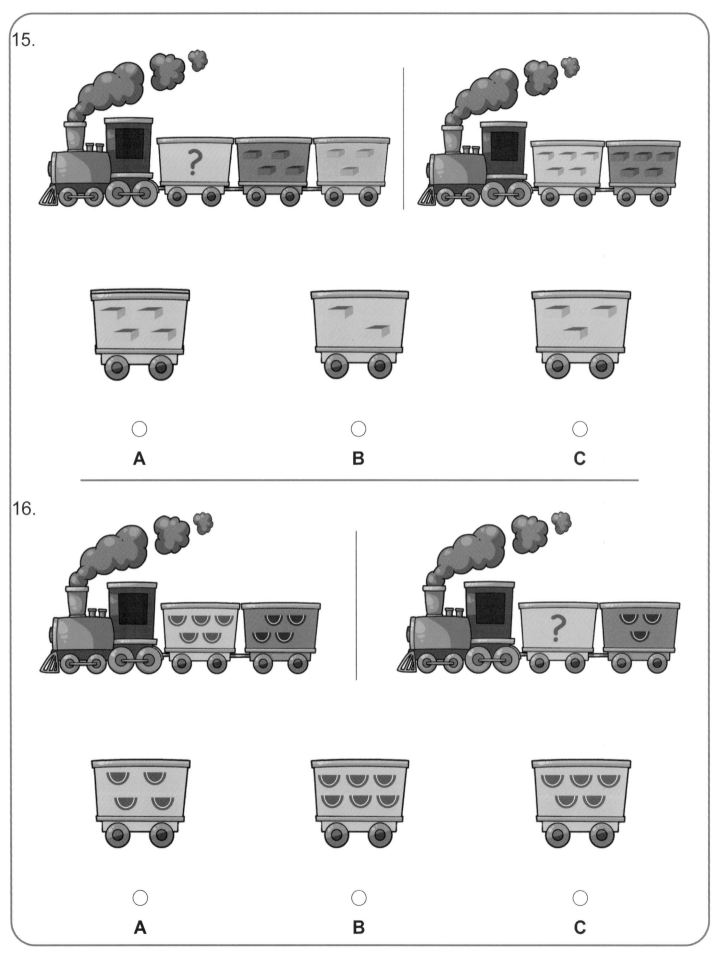

A   B   C

16.

A   B   C

Subset 6: Number Series

Instructions:

For each of the questions in this subset, you will see an abacus with some pattern represented by the number of beads in the rods. From the answer options provided to you, you need to find the rod with beads that when replaced with the empty rod in the abacus (shown by a "?") completes the pattern. Color the bubble under one option (A,B, or C) that is the best match.

The first two questions are samples and have been solved for you.

1.

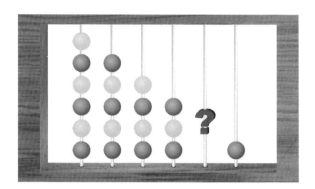   

                      A   **B**   **C**

C is correct. Your job is to find the option that has the rod with beads that best fit in the missing rod in the abacus in question (shown by a **"?"**). The pattern (from left to right) in the abacus shows rods with beads in descending order of numbers where each rod after the first carries one bead less than the rod on its left. Only C completes this pattern and is the correct answer.

2.

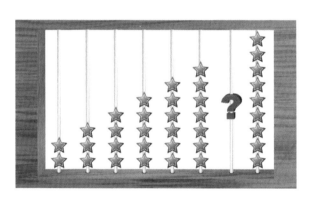   

                      A   **B**   **C**

A is correct. Your job is to find the option that has the rod with beads that best fit in the missing rod in the abacus in question (shown by a **"?"**). The pattern (from left to right) in the abacus shows rods with beads in ascending order of numbers where each rod after the first carries one bead more than the rod on its left. Only A completes this pattern and is the correct answer.

3.

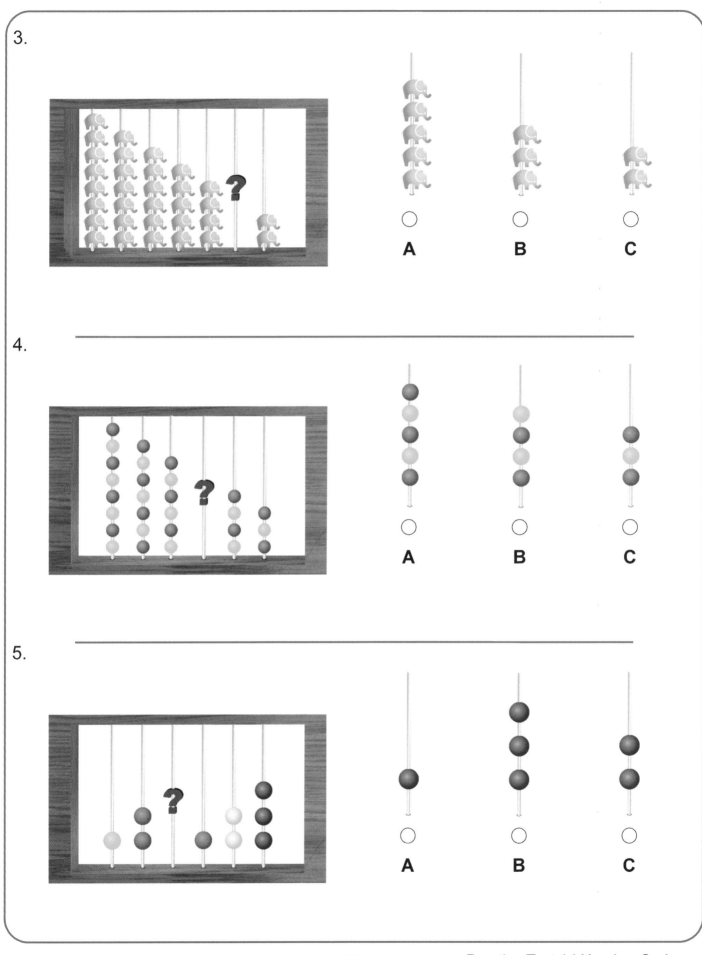

4.

5.

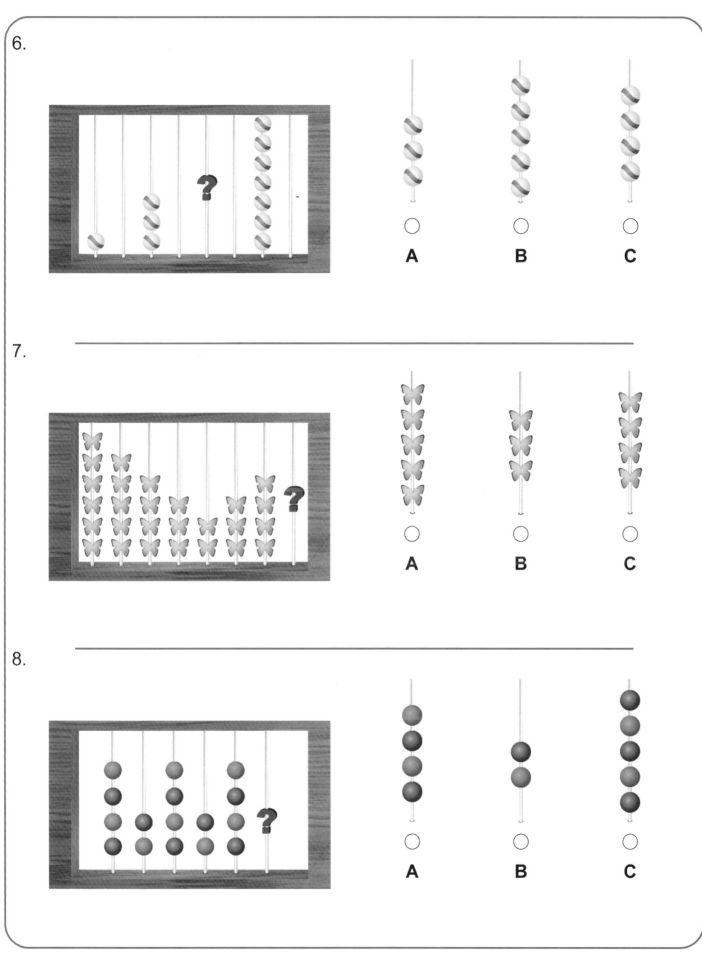

6.

7.

8.

9.

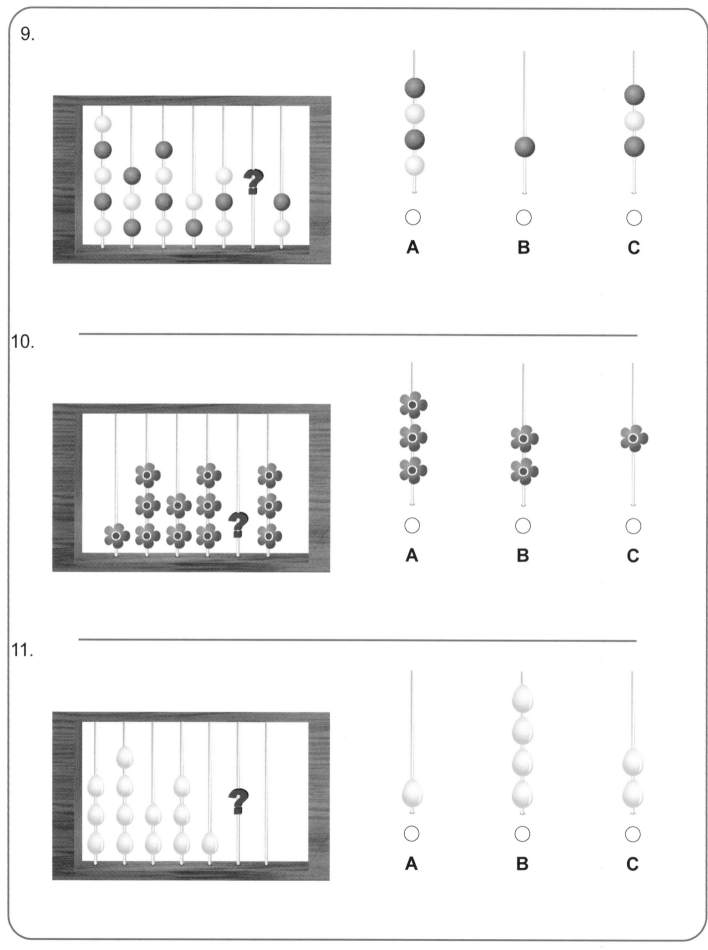

10.

11.

12.

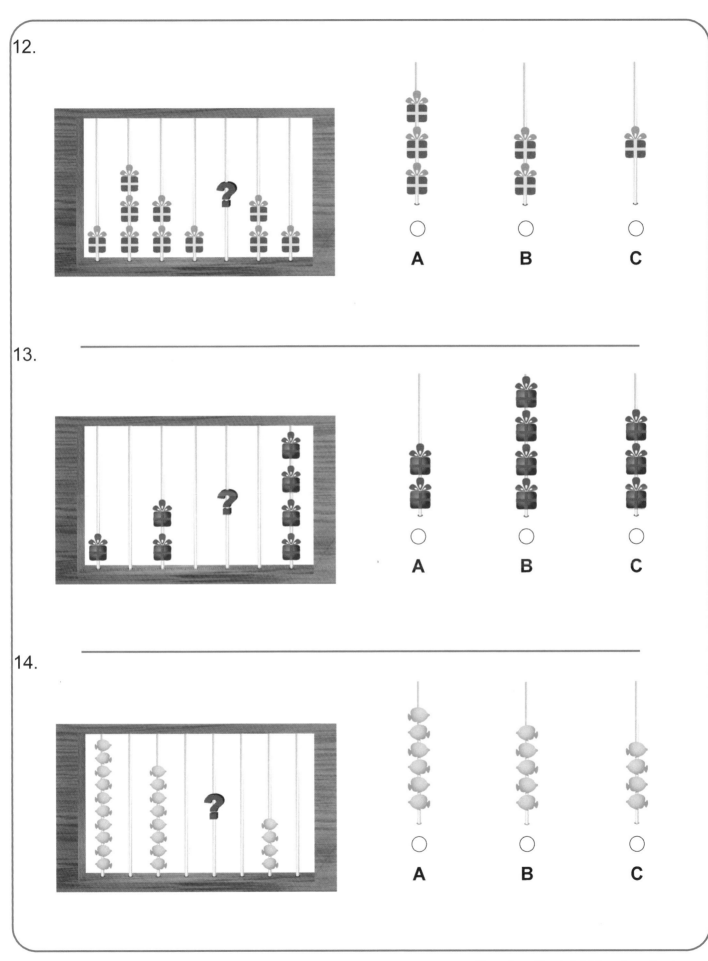

13.

14.

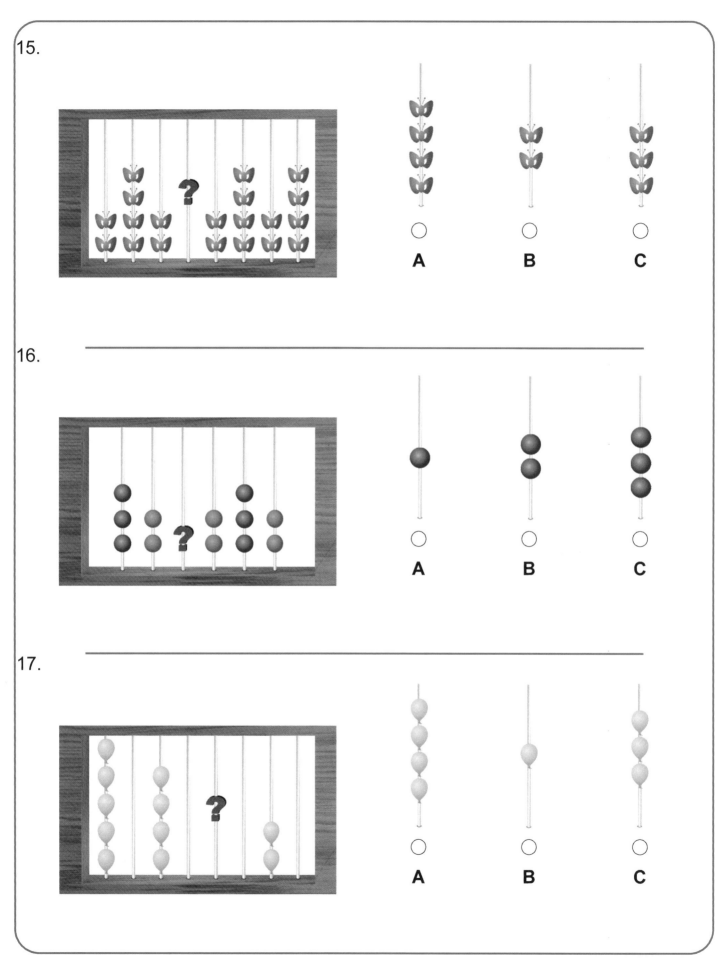

15.

16.

17.

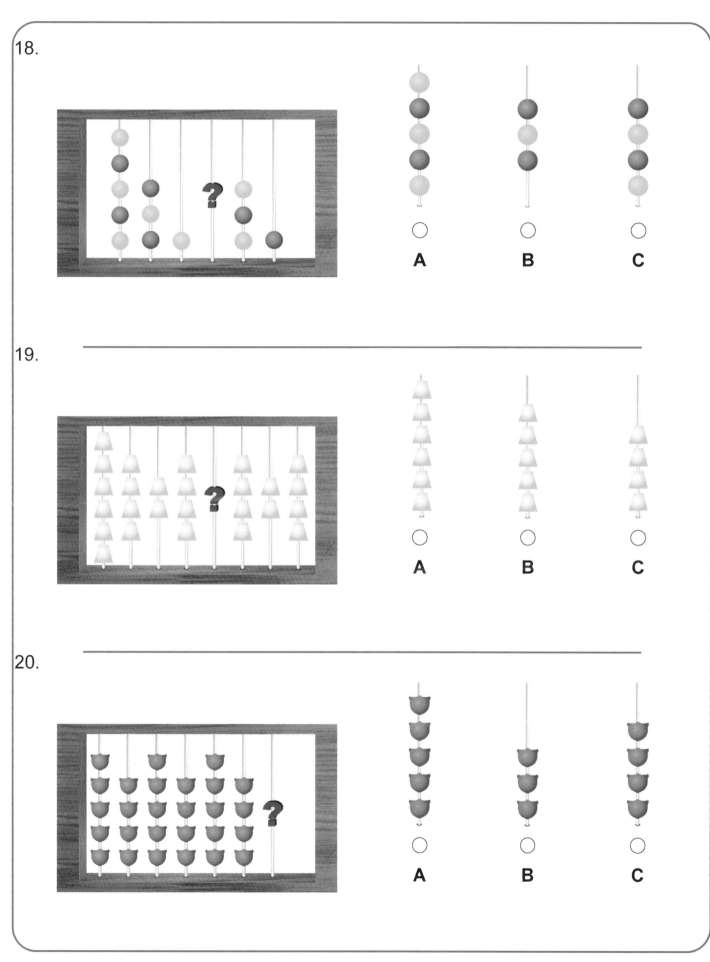

18.

19.

20.

Subset 7: Figure Matrices

Instructions:

For each of the questions in this subset, you have to first determine the relationship between the two figures in the top row. Next, look at the first figure in the bottom row and from the options provided to you, find the figure that best completes the relationship in the same way as the relationship between the two figures in the top row. Color the bubble under one option (A,B, or C) that is the best match.

The first two questions are samples and have been solved for you.

1.

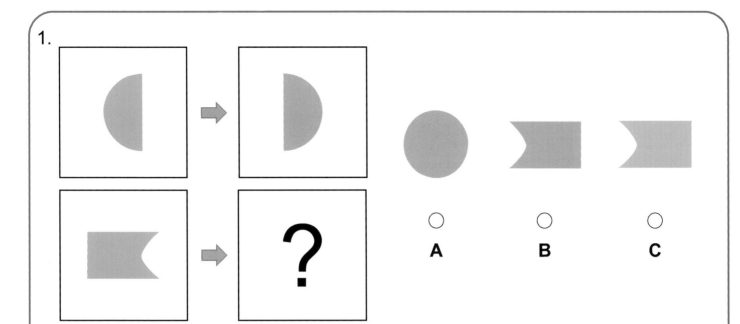

B is correct. Your job is to find the option that best fits the empty box in the bottom row (shown by a "?"). The two pictures in the top row show a relationship – the picture to the right is a blue-colored mirror image of the picture to the left. The bottom row should exhibit the same relationship. Only B is the blue-colored mirror image of the picture on the left side in the bottom row and is the correct answer.

2.

C is correct. Your job is to find the option that best fits the empty box in the bottom row (shown by a "?"). The two pictures in the top row show a relationship – on the right there is a white pentagon inside a yellow circle and on the left there is a white circle inside a yellow pentagon. The bottom row should exhibit the same relationship. Only C completes the relationship and is the correct answer.

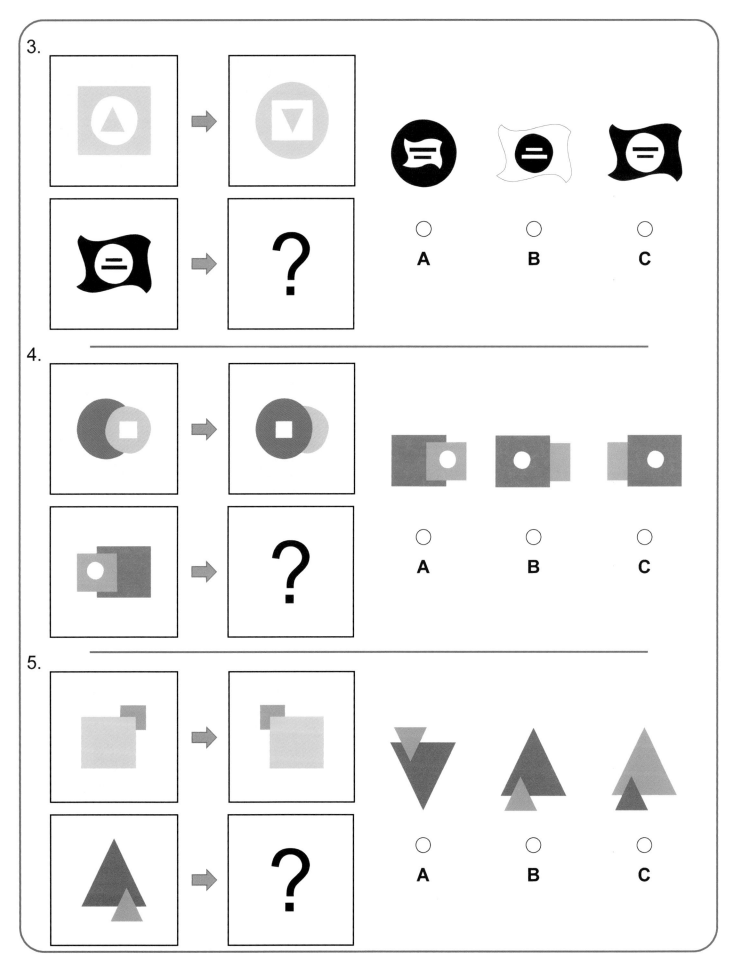

3.

4.

5.

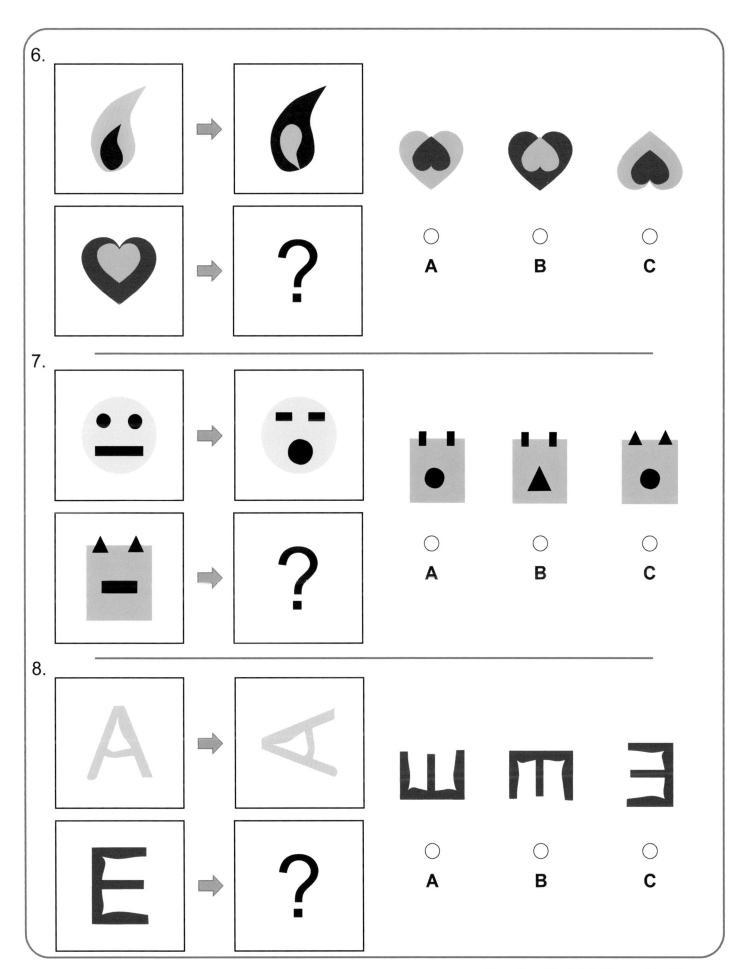

6.

7.

8.

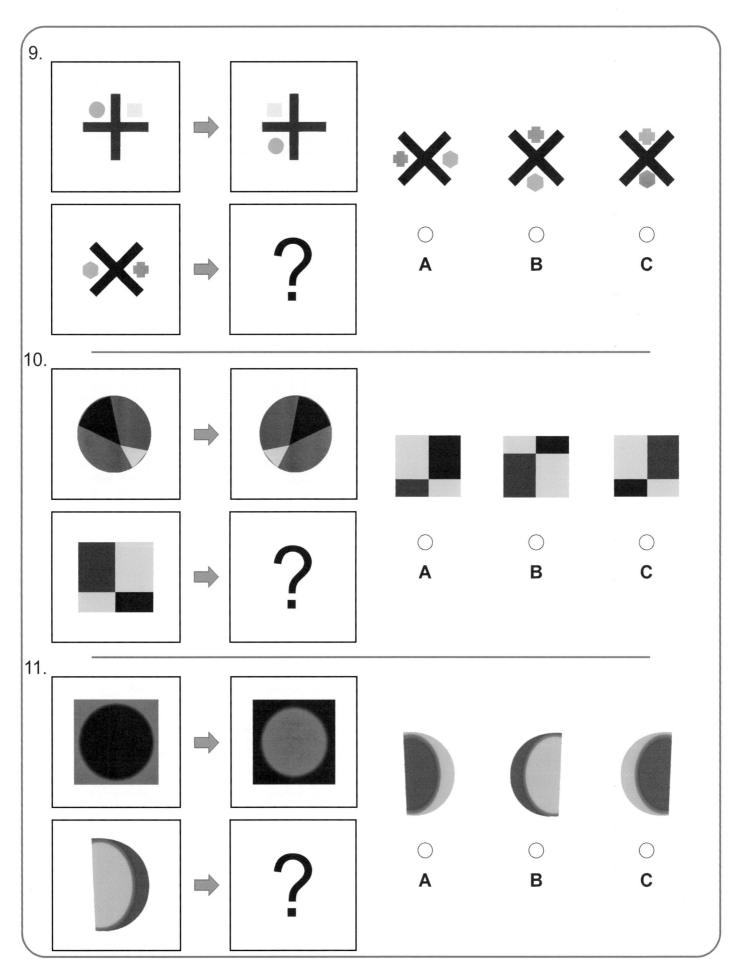

9.

10.

11.

Practice Test 1 | Figure Matrices

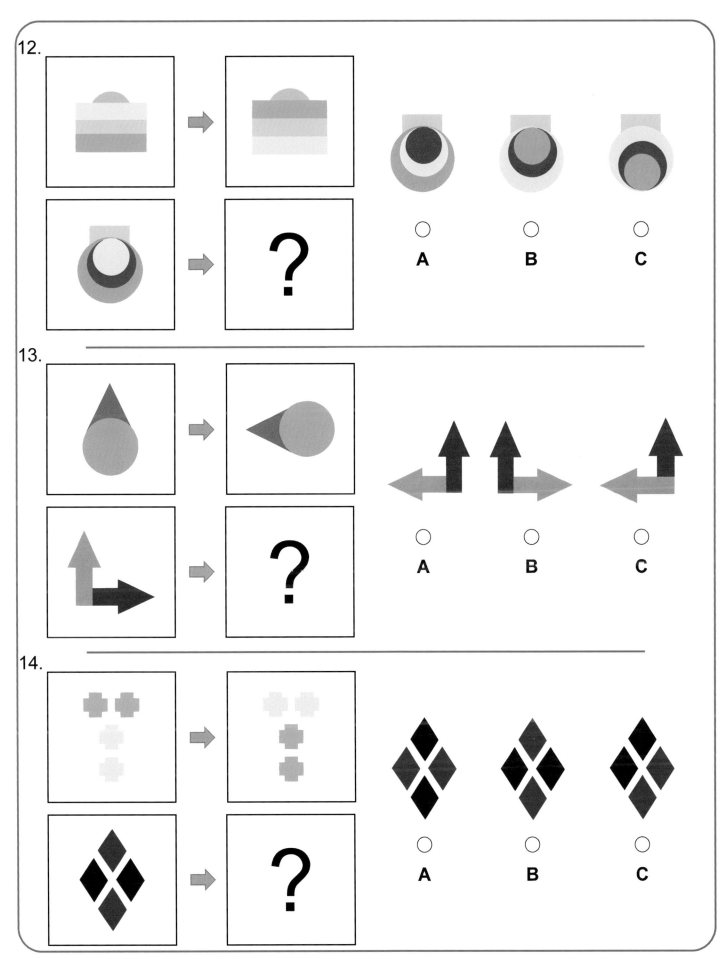

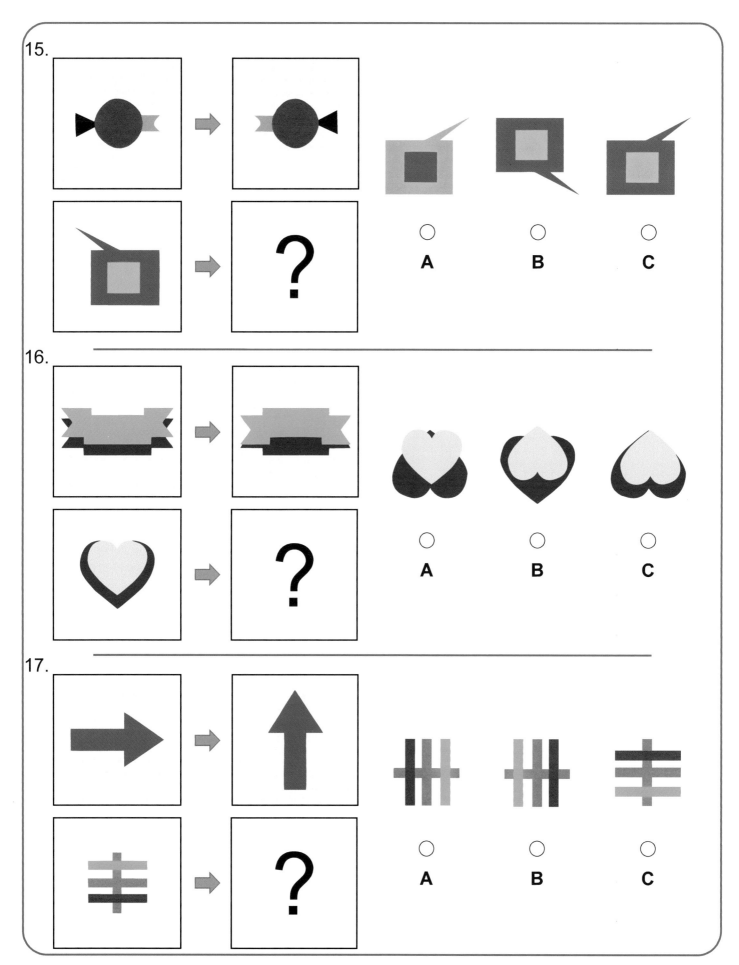

Practice Test 1 | Figure Matrices

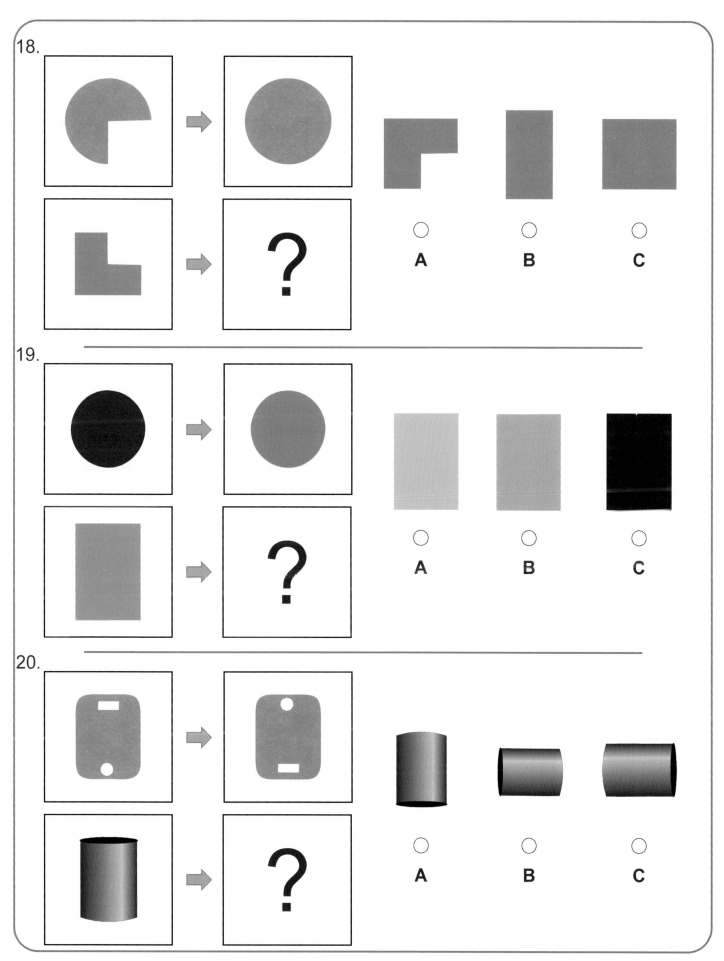

Subset 8: Paper Folding

Instructions:

For each of the questions in this subset, you will see a piece of paper that has been folded along a line shown and then has been either cut with a pair of scissors or has holes punched through it. From the answer options provided to you, you need to find the option that best shows how the paper will look when it is unfolded. Color the bubble under one option (A,B, or C) that is the best match.

The first two questions are samples and have been solved for you.

1.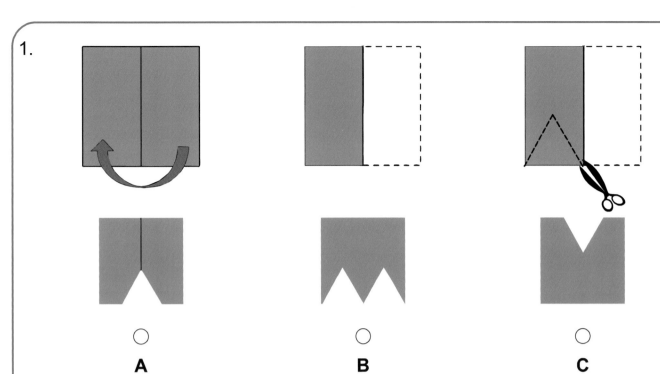

          A   B   C

B is correct. In the question, the flow of pictures from left to right shows you how a piece of paper is folded along a solid line and then cut with a pair of scissors. Your job is to find the option that shows how the paper will look when it is unfolded. Only B shows accurately how the unfolded paper will look and is the correct answer.

2.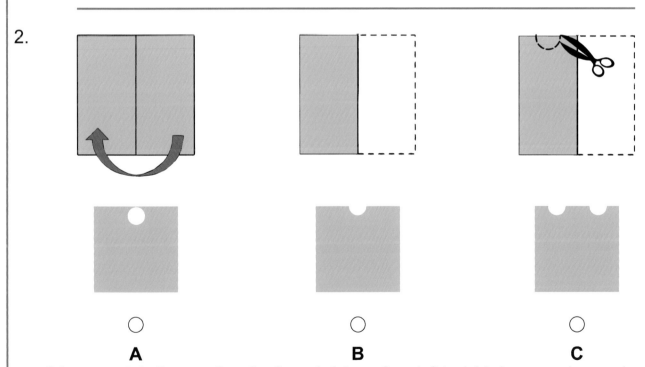

          A   B   C

C is correct. In the question, the flow of pictures from left to right shows you how a piece of paper is folded along a solid line and then cut with a pair of scissors. Your job is to find the option that shows how the paper will look when it is unfolded. Only C shows accurately how the unfolded paper will look and is the correct answer.

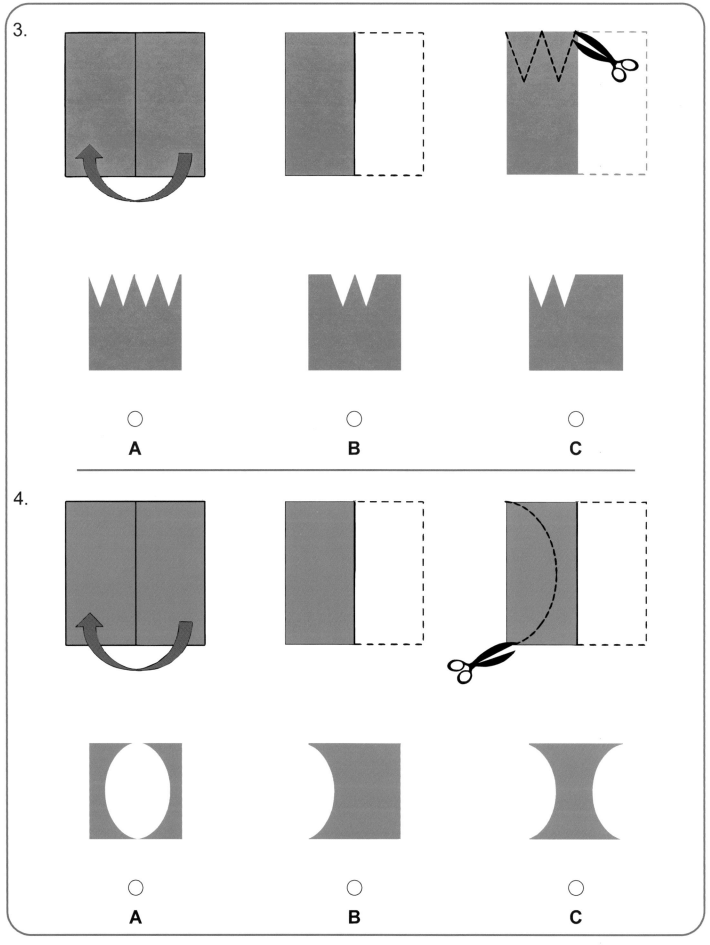

3.

○ A

○ B

○ C

4.

○ A

○ B

○ C

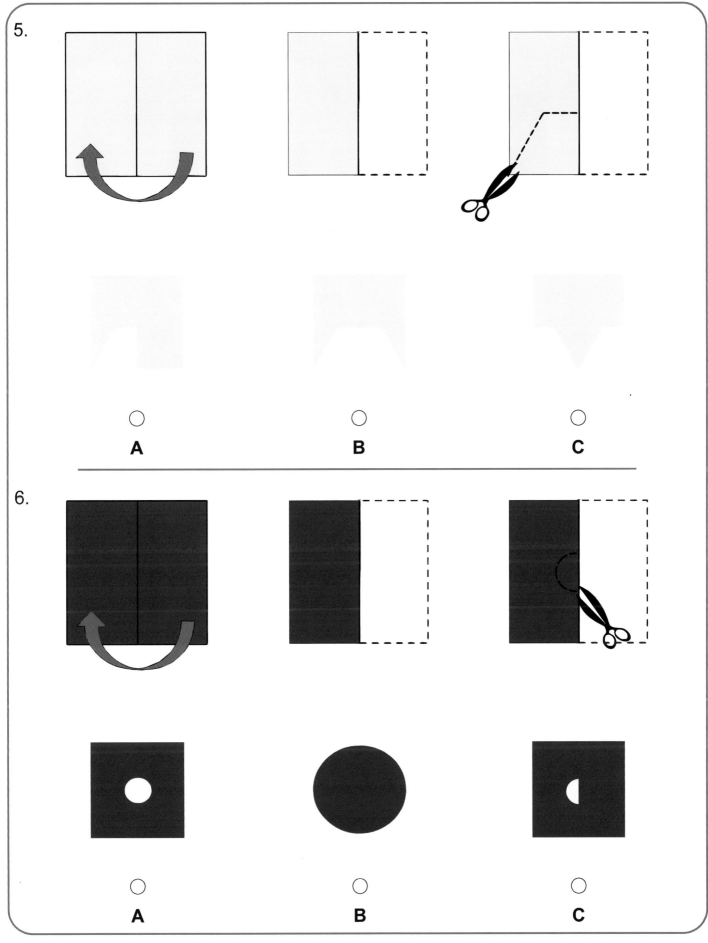

5.

A ○
B ○
C ○

6.

A ○
B ○
C ○

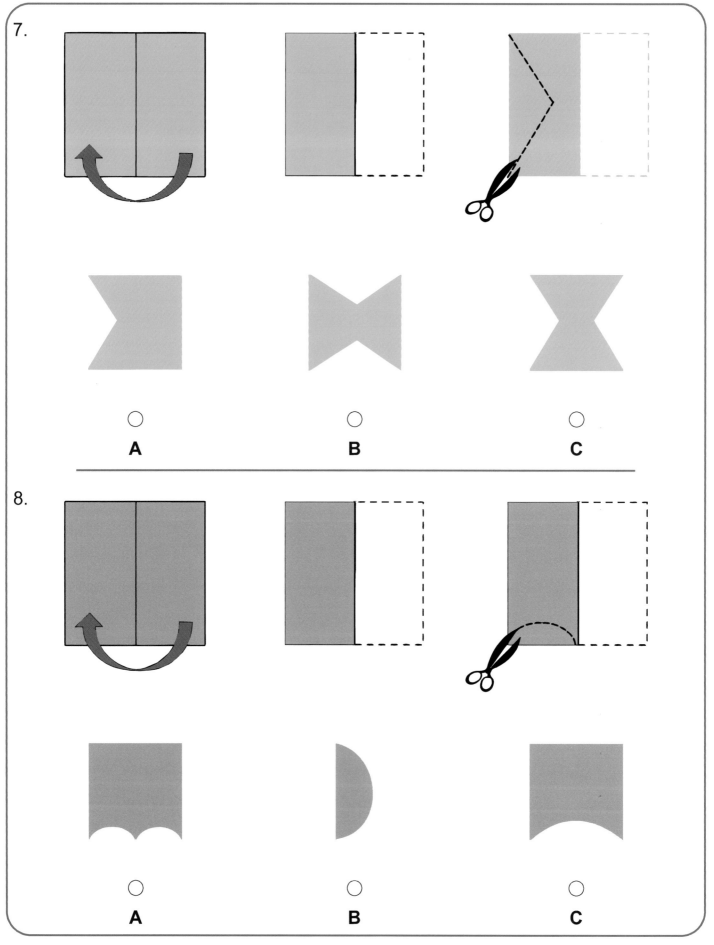

7.

A

B

C

8.

A

B

C

9.

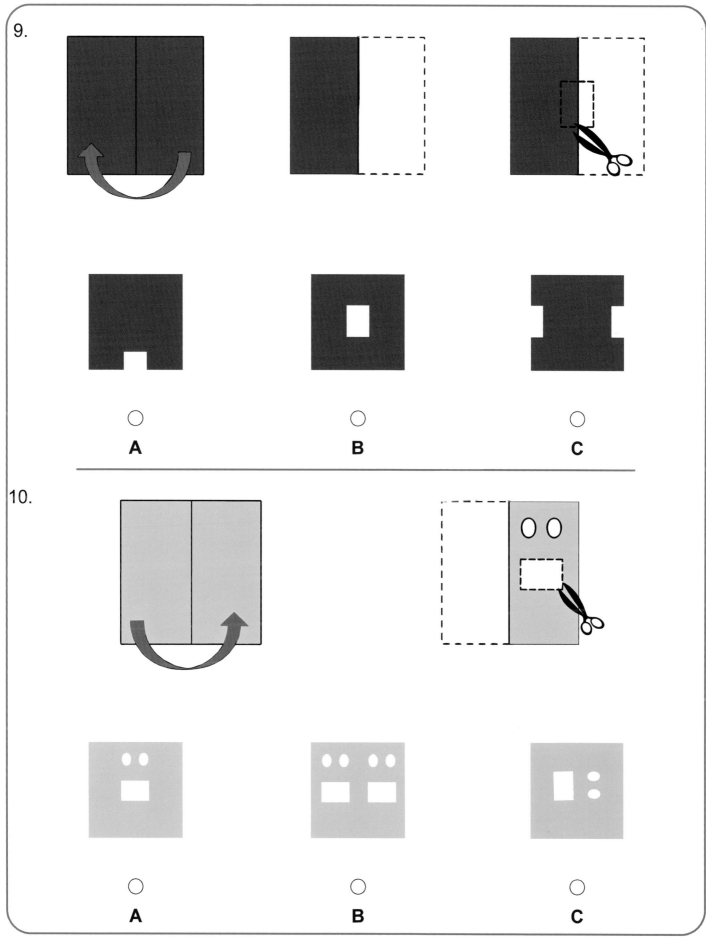

○
A

○
B

○
C

10.

○
A

○
B

○
C

11.

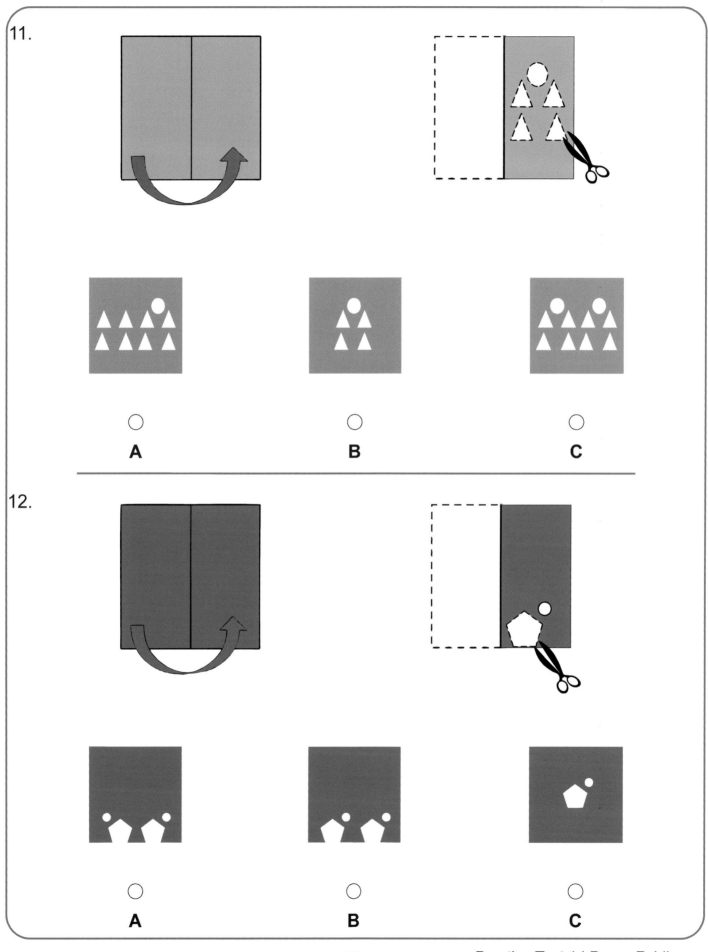

A

B

C

12.

A

B

C

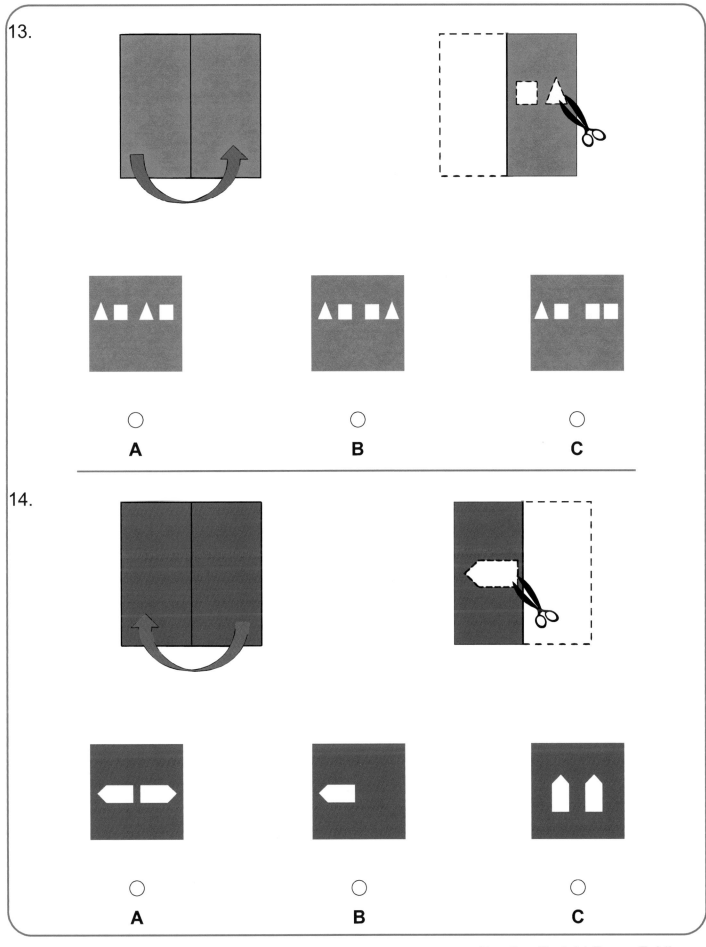

15.

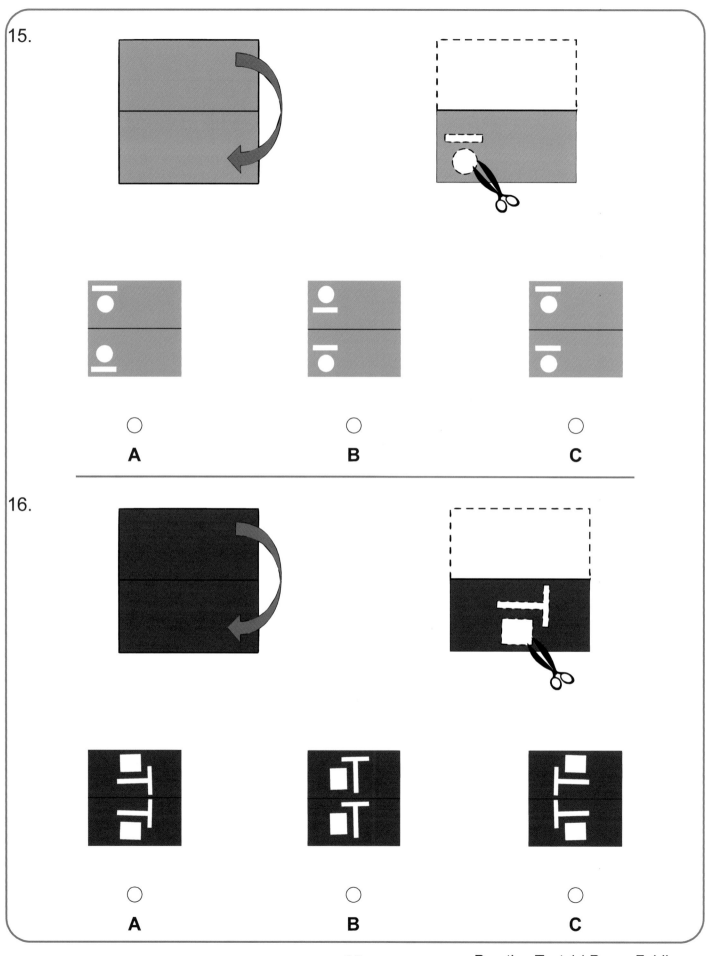

A

B

C

16.

A

B

C

Subset 9: Figure Classification

Instructions:

For each of the questions in this subset, first look at the three figures on the left side of the line and determine how they are similar. Next, look at the figures on the right side of the line and color the bubble under one option (A,B, or C) that is the best match.

The first two questions are samples and have been solved for you.

1.

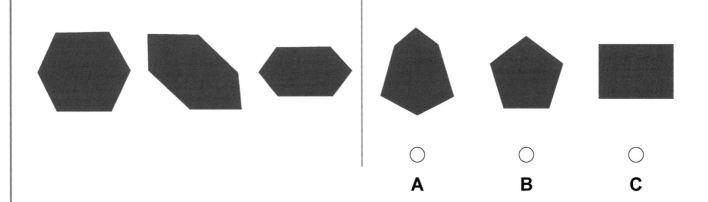

○	○	○
A	**B**	**C**

A is correct. Your job is to find the option with the picture that most closely resembles the three pictures on the left. All the pictures on the left have six sides. Only A has six sides and is the correct answer.

2.

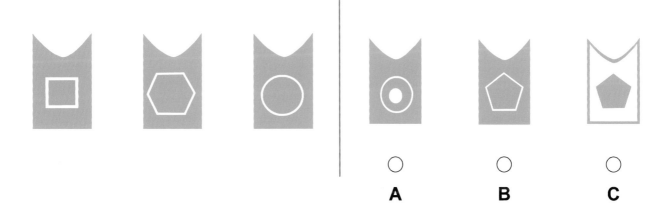

○	○	○
A	**B**	**C**

B is correct. Your job is to find the option with the picture that most closely resembles the three pictures on the left. All the pictures on the left have a single geometrical figure inside a green colored object. Only B has a single geometrical figure inside a green colored object and is the correct answer.

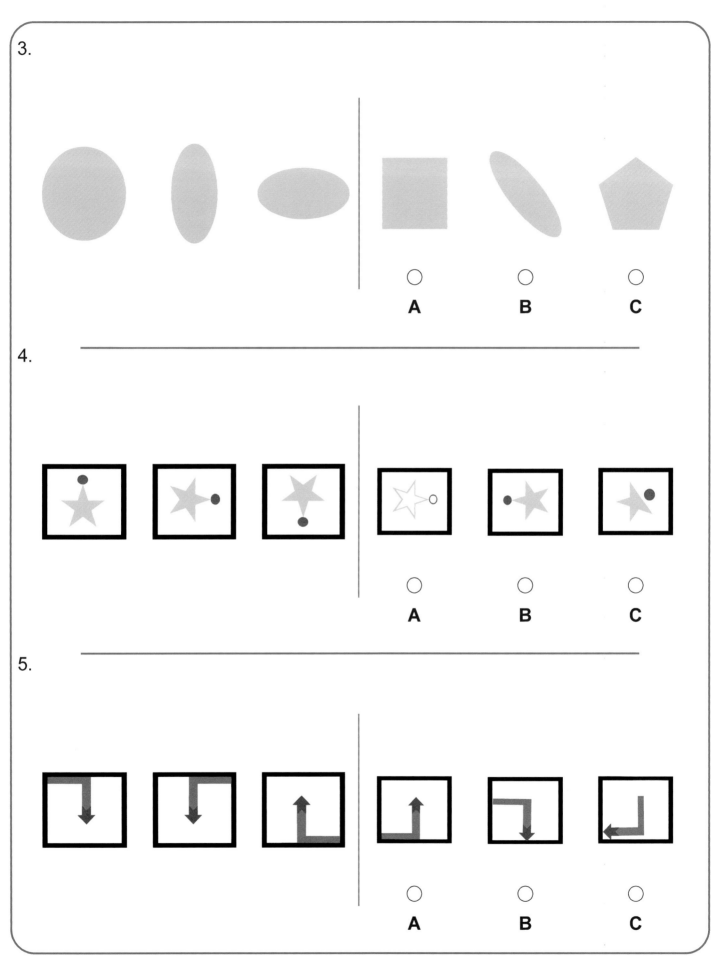

3.

A
B
C

4.

A
B
C

5.

A
B
C

6.

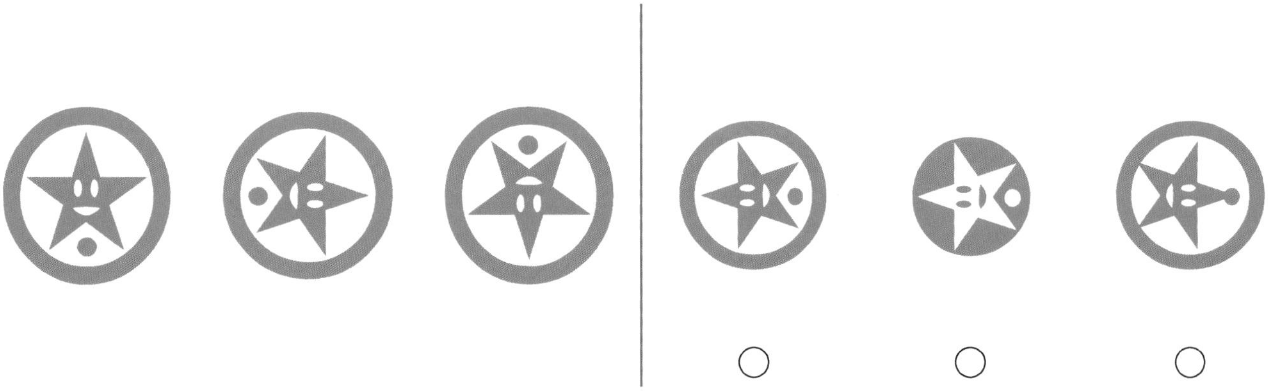

○ **A** ○ **B** ○ **C**

7.

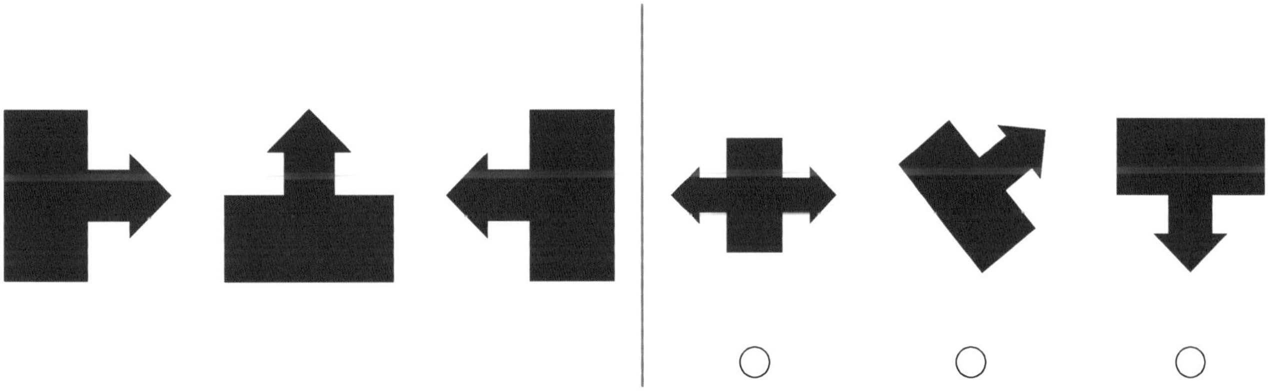

○ **A** ○ **B** ○ **C**

8.

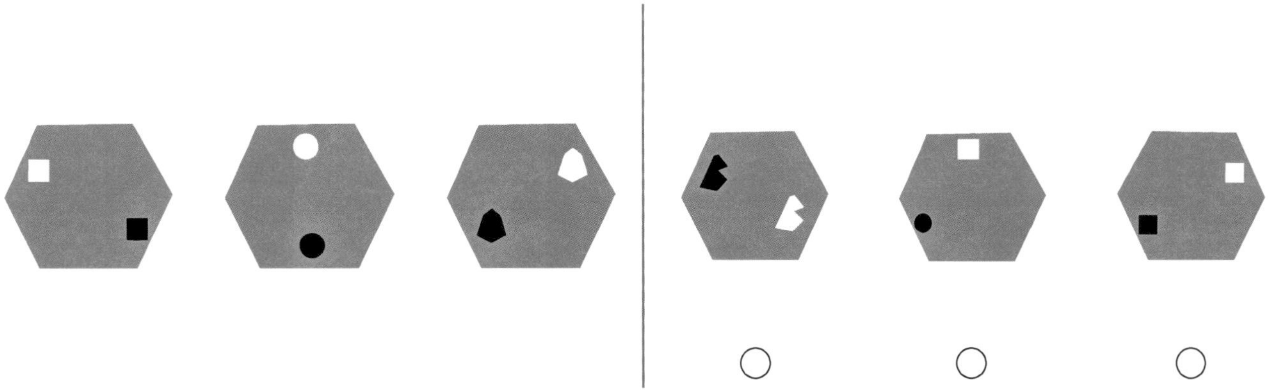

○ **A** ○ **B** ○ **C**

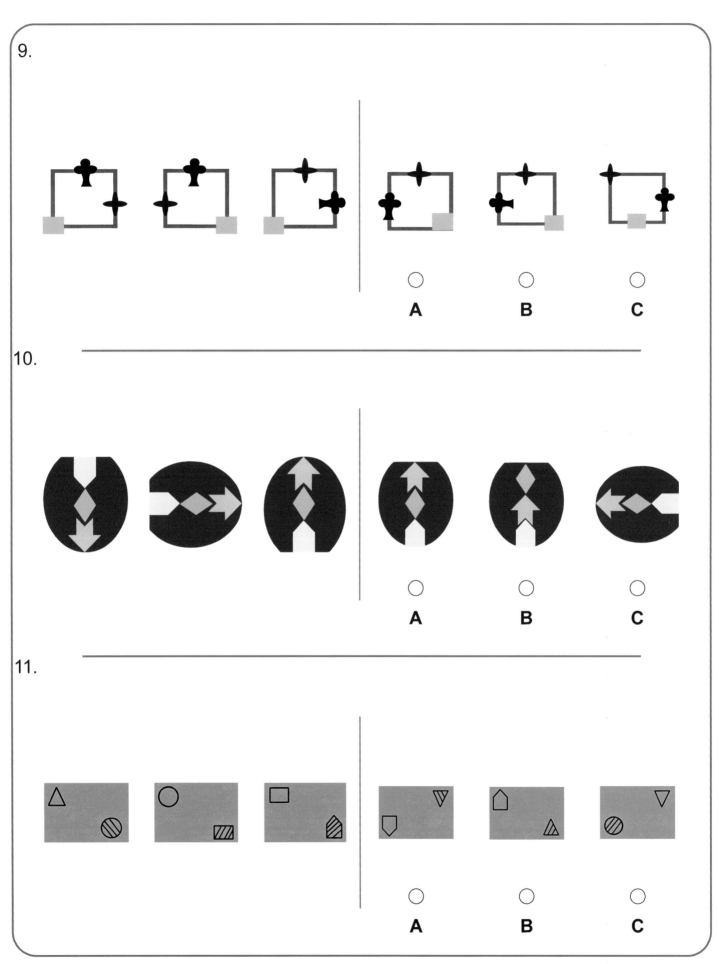

9.

A   B   C

10.

A   B   C

11.

A   B   C

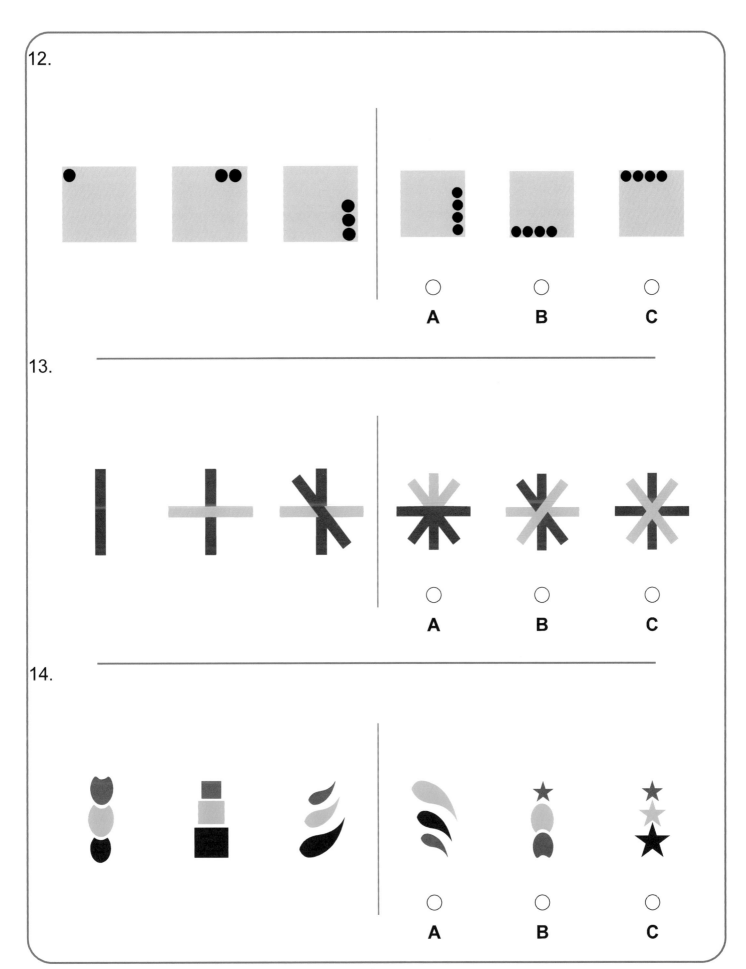

12.

A ○
B ○
C ○

13.

A ○
B ○
C ○

14.

A ○
B ○
C ○

15.

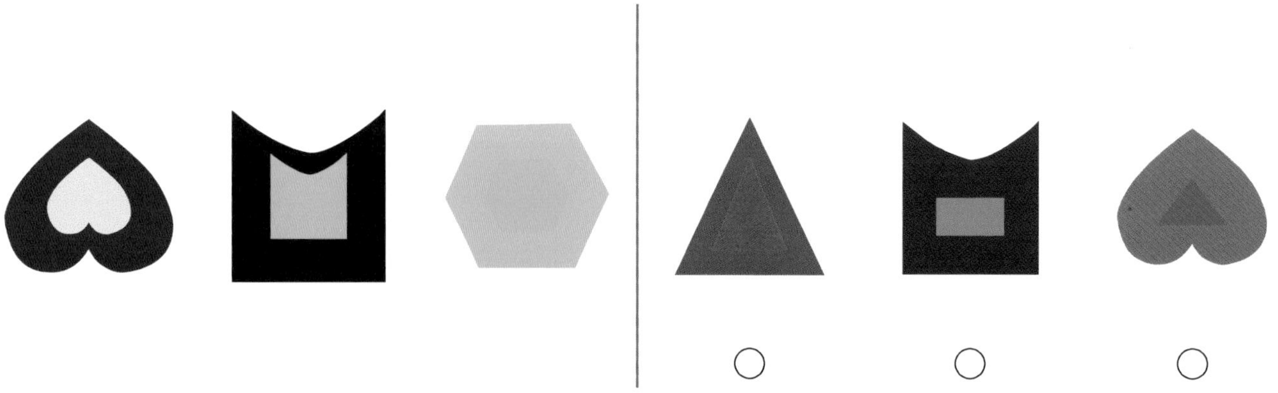

○   ○   ○
A   **B**   **C**

16.

○   ○   ○
A   **B**   **C**

17.

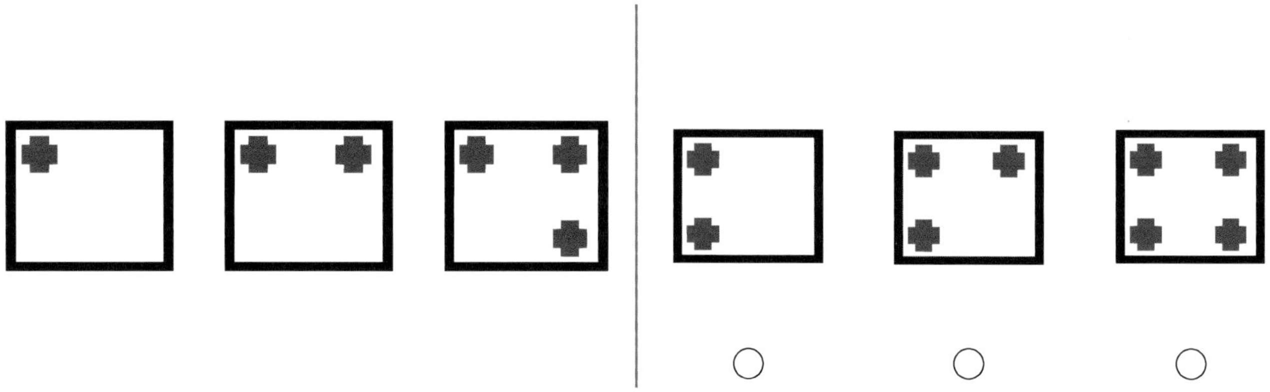

○   ○   ○
A   **B**   **C**

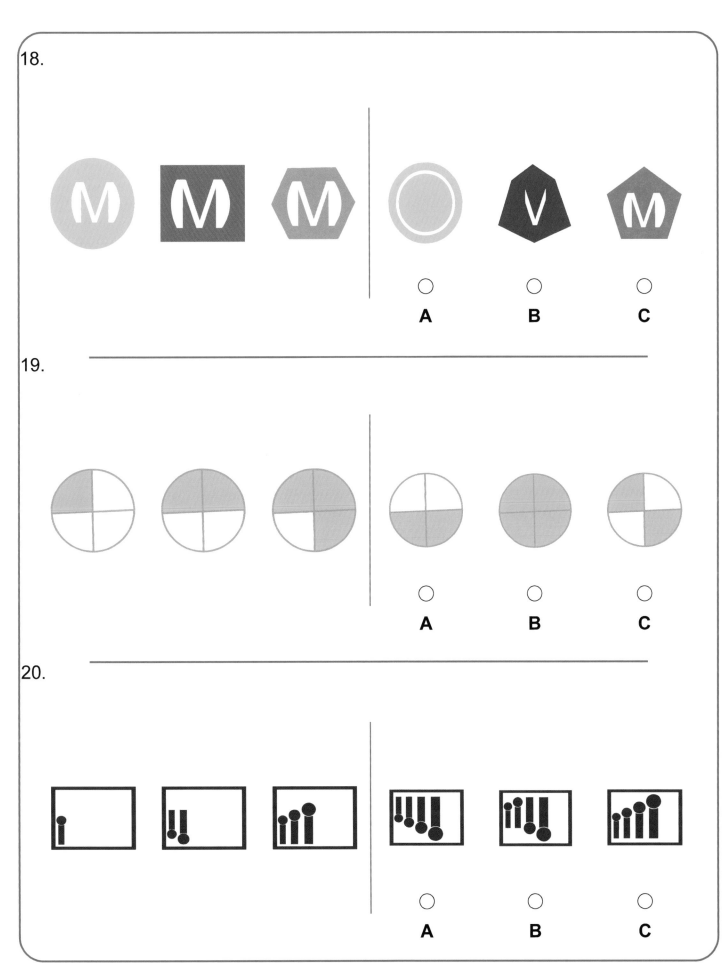

18.

A B C

19.

A B C

20.

A B C

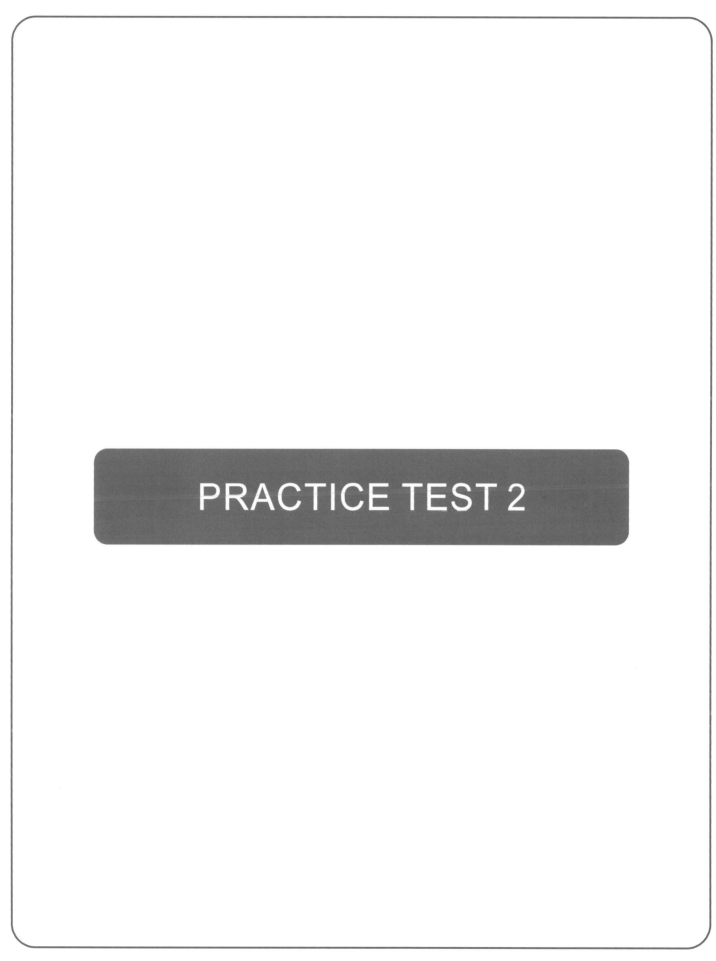

PRACTICE TEST 2

Subset 1: Picture Analogies

Instructions:

For each of the questions in this subset, you have to first determine the relationship between the two pictures in the top row. Next, look at the first picture in the bottom row and from the options provided to you, find the picture that best completes the relationship in the same way as the relationship between the two pictures in the top row. Color the bubble under one option (A,B, or C) that is the best match.

The first two questions are samples and have been solved for you.

1.

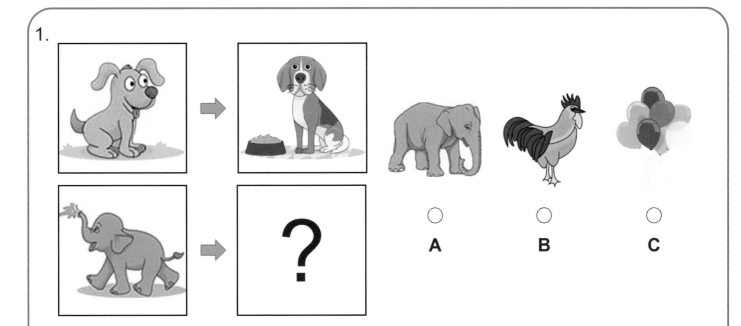

A is correct. Your aim is to find the option that best fits the empty box in the bottom row shown by "?". The two pictures in the top row show a relationship between a puppy and a dog. The puppy grows up to become a dog. The first picture in the bottom row is an elephant calf and is supposed to be related in the same way (as the pictures in top row) to one of the pictures in options A,B, and C. Option B is incorrect because an elephant calf can't grow up to become a hen. Answer C is also incorrect because an elephant calf can't grow up to become a bunch of balloons! The elephant calf can only grow up to become an elephant, which is option A.

2.

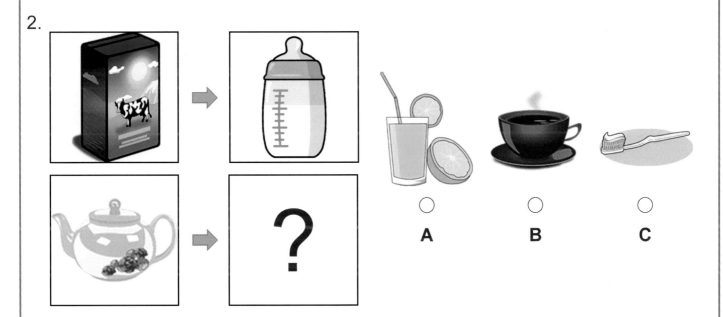

B is correct. Your aim is to find the option that best fits the empty box in the bottom row shown by "?". The two pictures in the top row show a relationship between a milk carton and an infant's milk bottle. The carton contains the milk that fills the milk bottle. The first picture in the bottom row is a kettle and is supposed to be related in the same way (as the pictures in top row) to one of the pictures in options A,B, and C. Option A is incorrect because a kettle most likely does not contain orange juice! Answer C is also incorrect because a kettle does not contain toothpaste! The kettle can contain hot tea or coffee that can fill a cup, which is option B.

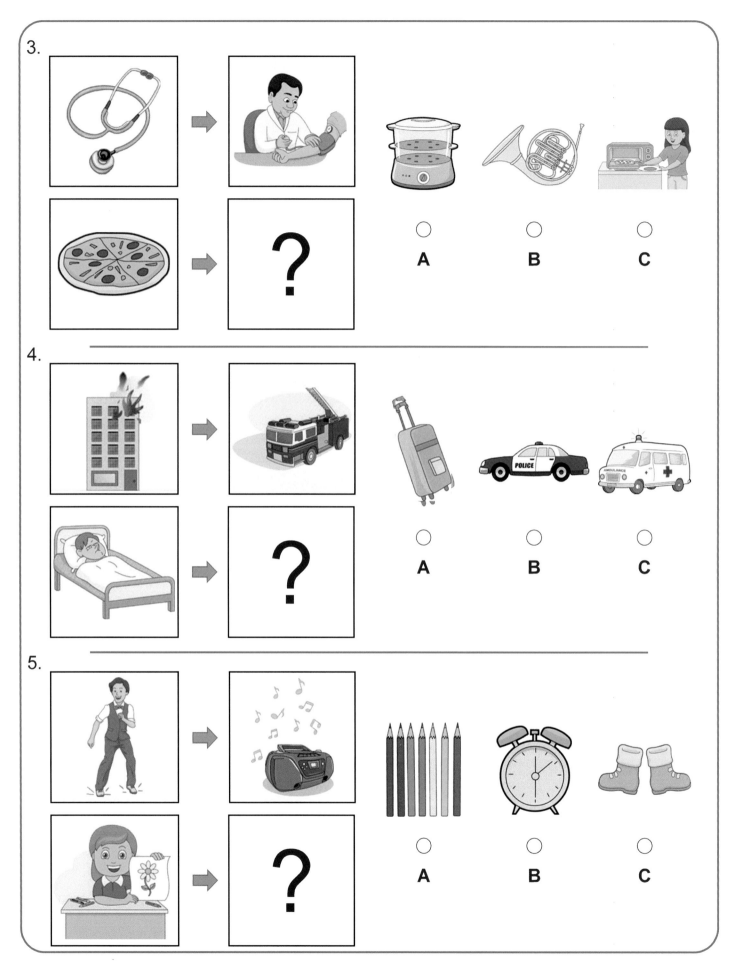

Practice Test 2 | Picture Analogies

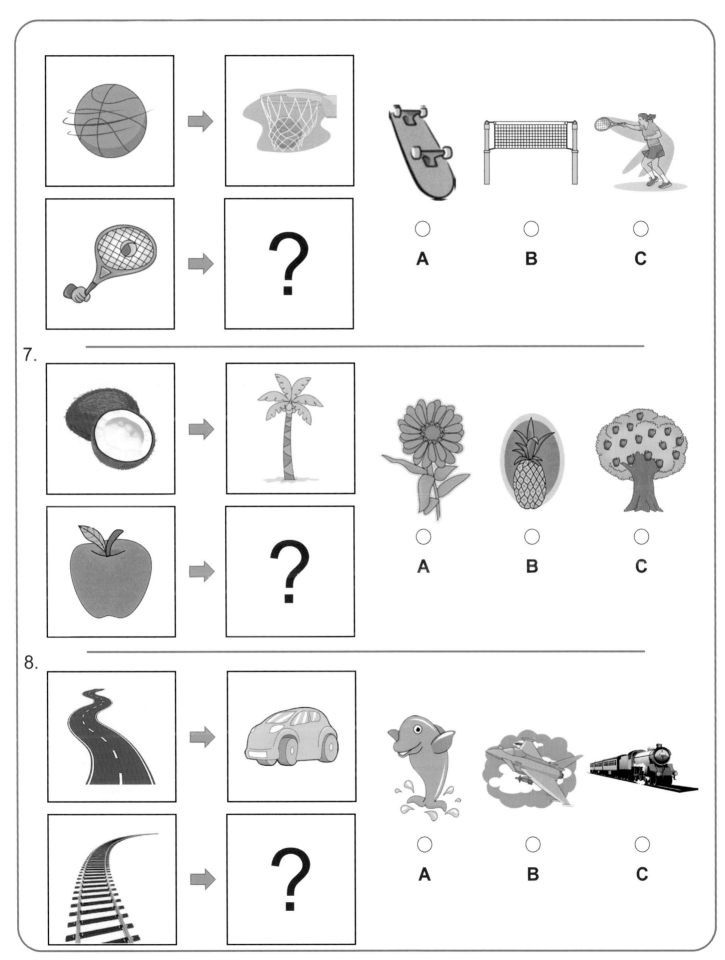

7.

8.

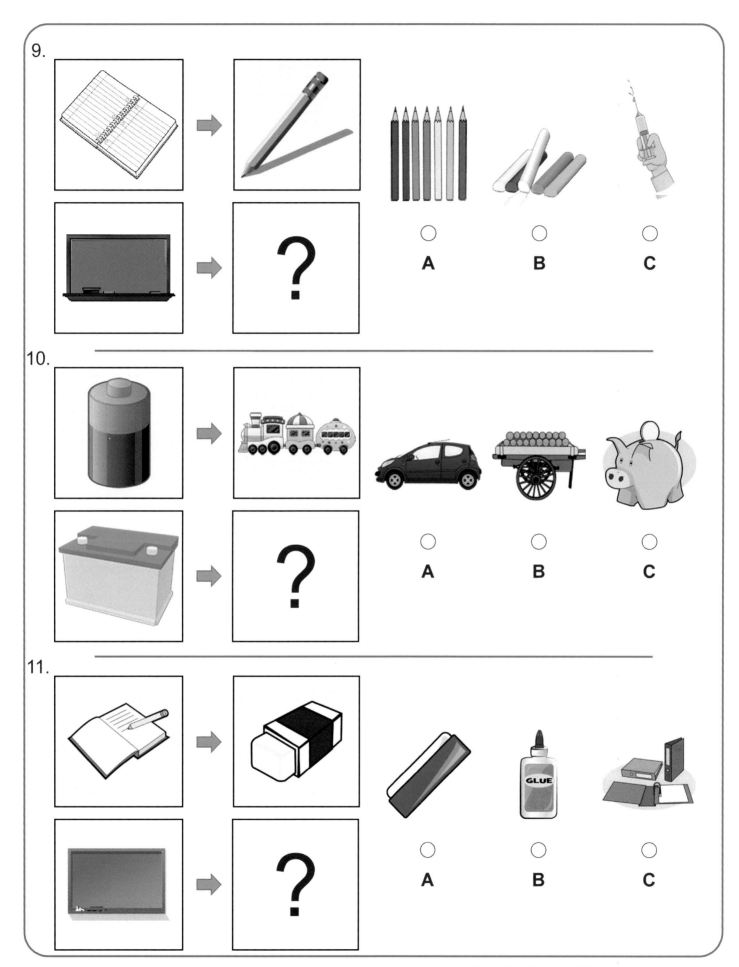

Practice Test 2 | Picture Analogies

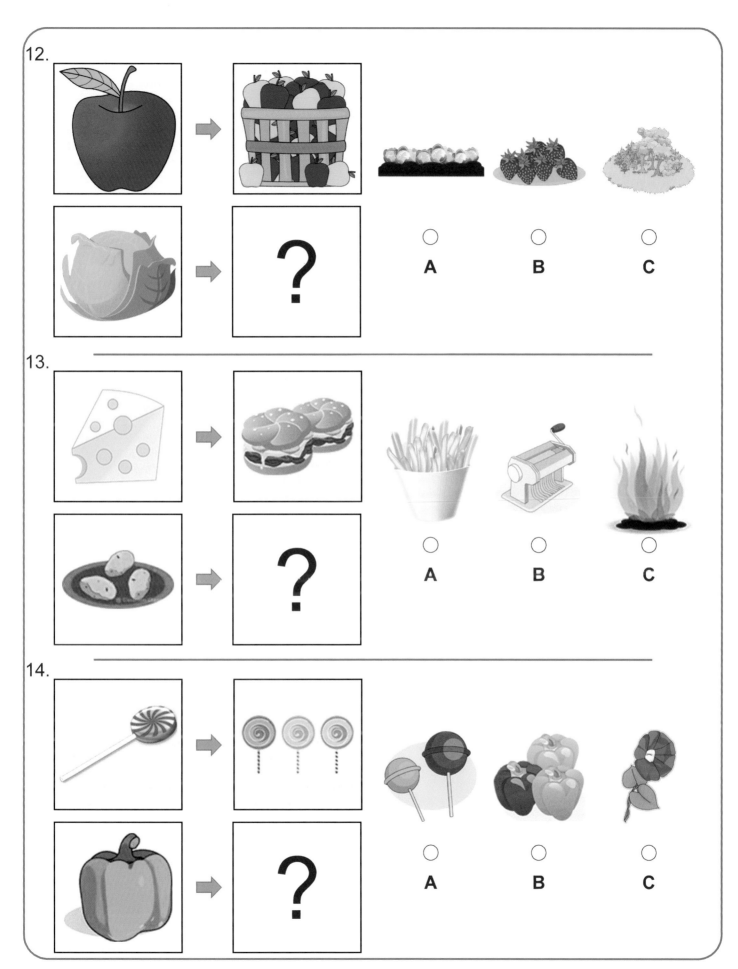

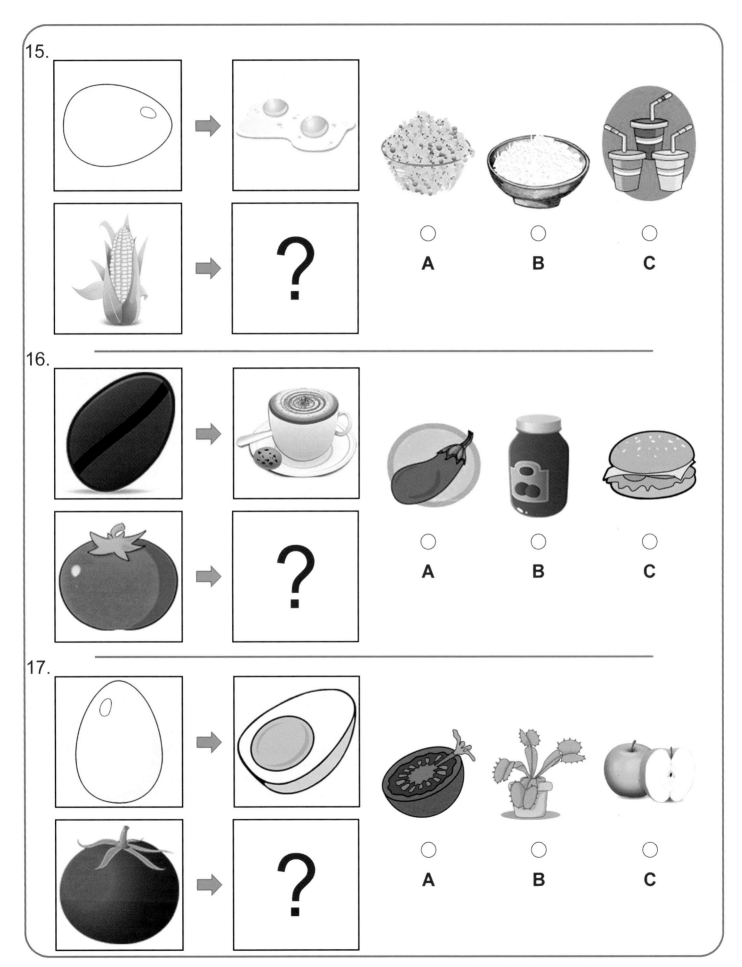

Practice Test 2 | Picture Analogies

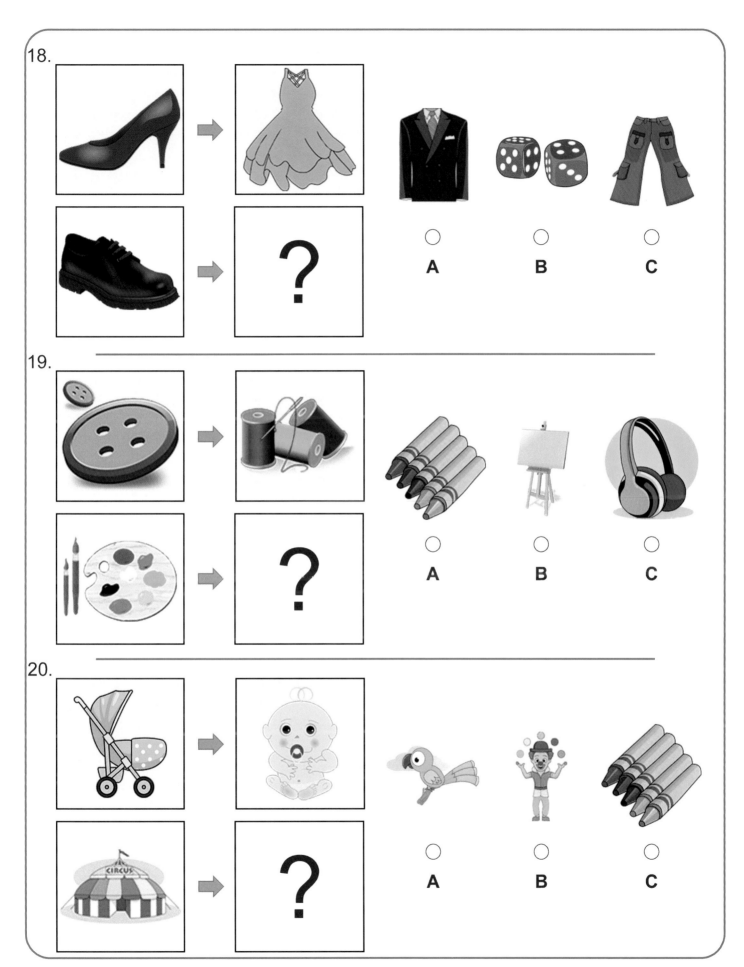

Subset 2: Sentence Completion

Instructions:

In the primary edition (grades K to 2 / levels 5/6 to 8), the questions in this subset will be read out to you by the teacher or the administrator. Listen to what is read out very carefully as some of the sentences may have a 'not', 'non' or 'un-' words that reverse the meaning of the sentence.

For each of the questions in this subset, find the picture that best answers the sentence in the question. Color the bubble under one option (A,B, or C) that is the best match.

The first question is a sample and has been solved for you.

1. Which one of these is used for playing golf?

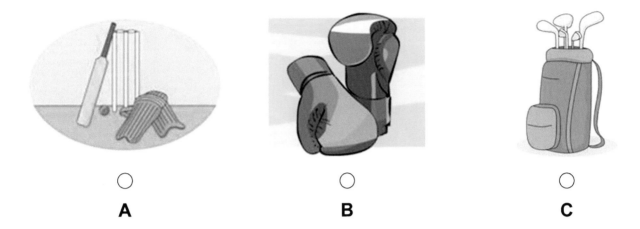

| A | B | C |

C is correct. A is incorrect because a cricket bat, ball, wickets, and pad are used to play cricket. B is also incorrect because boxing gloves are used to box. C is a golf kit that is used to play golf, the only correct option.

2. Which one of these is most likely a winter-wear?

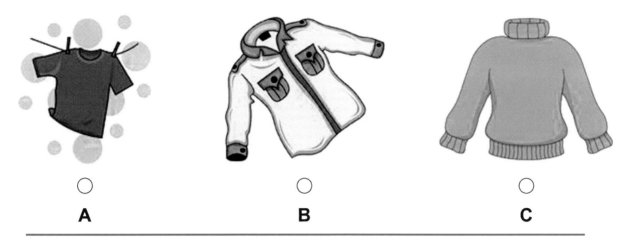

    ○   ○   ○

    A   B   C

3. Which one of these can be used to print images?

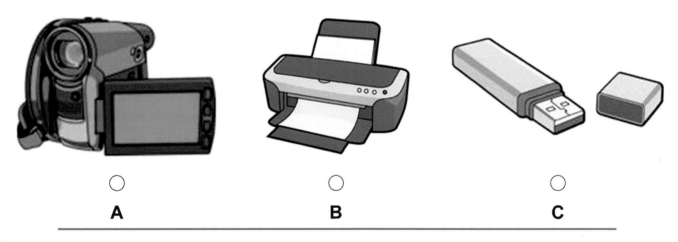

    ○   ○   ○

    A   B   C

4. Nicole is getting late for the party. She has just taken a shower, worn her dress, but her hair is still wet. Which one of these is Nicole most likely to use to be ready for the party quickly?

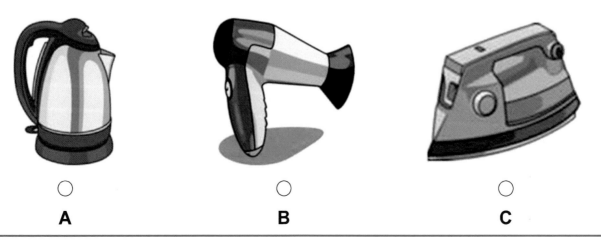

    ○   ○   ○

    A   B   C

5. Which one of these is most likely to be used by a watchman at night?

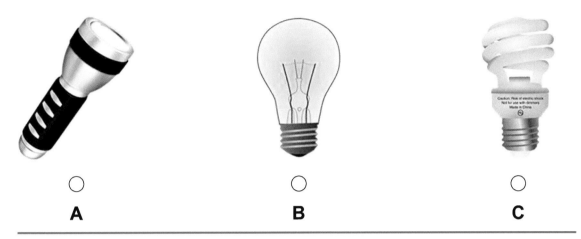

A   B   C

6. Which one of these has a pleasant fragrance?

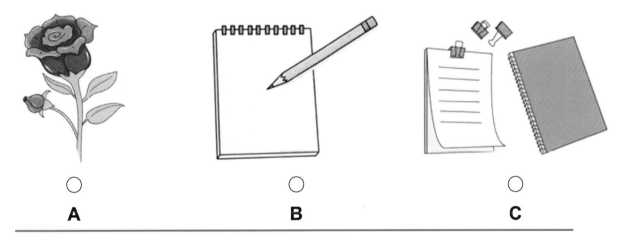

A   B   C

7. Who among these is not exercising?

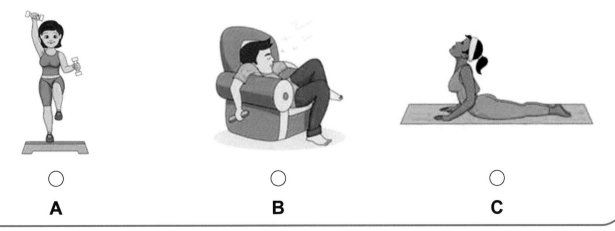

A   B   C

8. Which one of these pictures shows a child not in a playful mood?

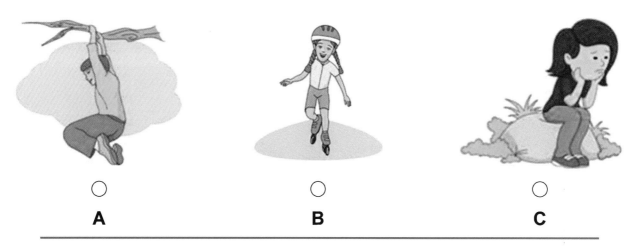

A

B

C

9. Nicky is fond of playing in water. Who among these is most likely to be Nicky?

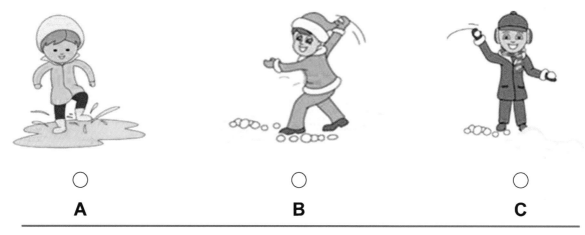

A

B

C

10. Which one of these pictures is most likely an example of strong wind that can blow you away?

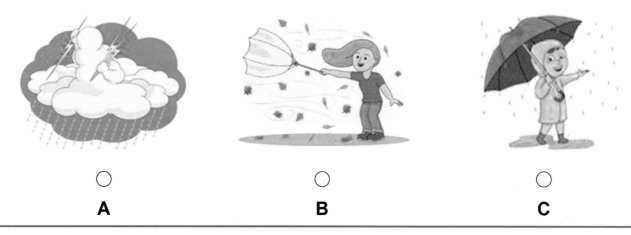

A

B

C

11. Which one of these is most likely unhealthy food?

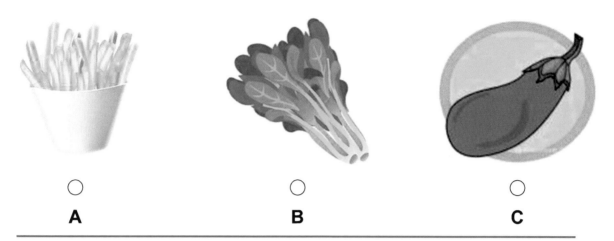

○ A   ○ B   ○ C

12. Which one of these fruits is likely to have the most water content?

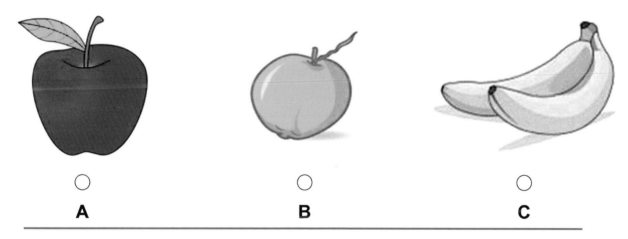

○ A   ○ B   ○ C

13. If you had to drink cold water, which one of these would you most likely use?

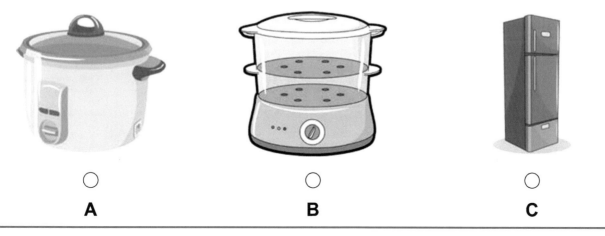

○ A   ○ B   ○ C

14. Which one of these is a mammal?

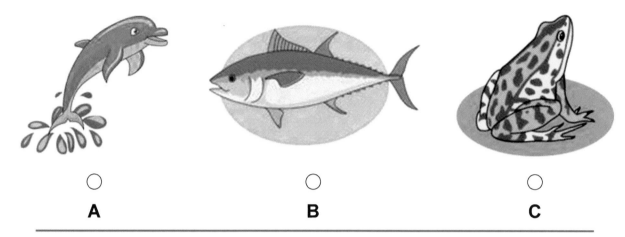

A   B   C

15. An animal with a beak. Which one of these is it?

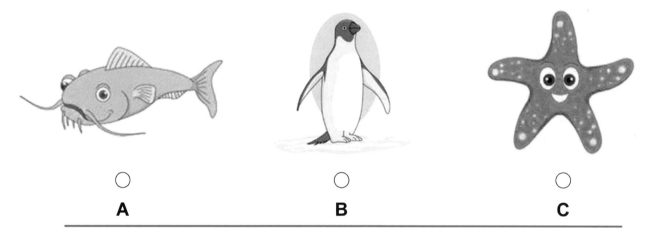

A   B   C

16. Which one of these can tell you the time?

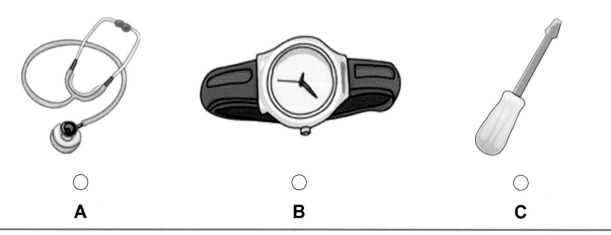

A   B   C

17. Mr. Walter, the baseball coach, has asked Adam to report to the training at 6 AM. Adam has a habit of waking up late. Which one of the instruments shown below should Adam use to ensure he wakes up on time for the baseball training?

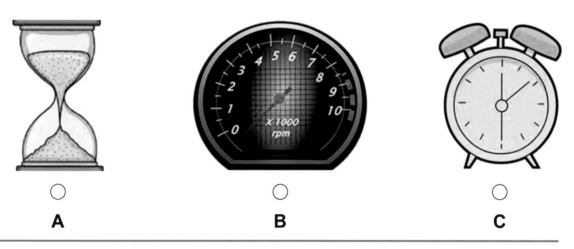

A   B   C

18. Which one of these can most likely float on water?

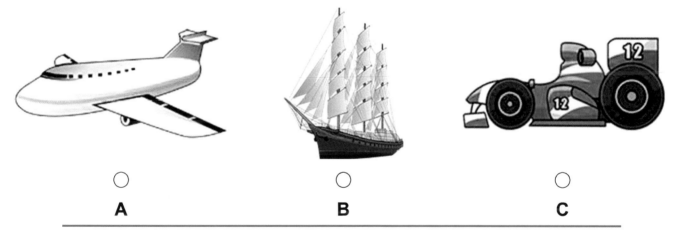

A   B   C

19. Which one of these picture is not in a group?

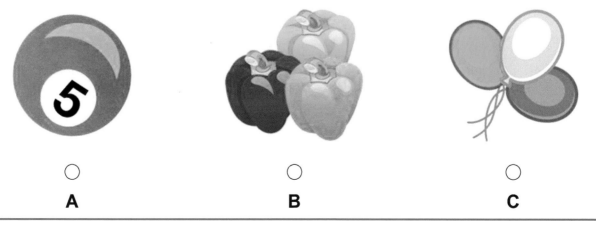

A   B   C

Subset 3: Picture Classification

Instructions:

For each of the questions in this subset, first look at the three pictures above the line and determine how they are similar as objects or activities. Next, look at the pictures below the line and color the bubble under one option (A,B, or C) that is the best match.

The first two questions are samples and have been solved for you.

1.

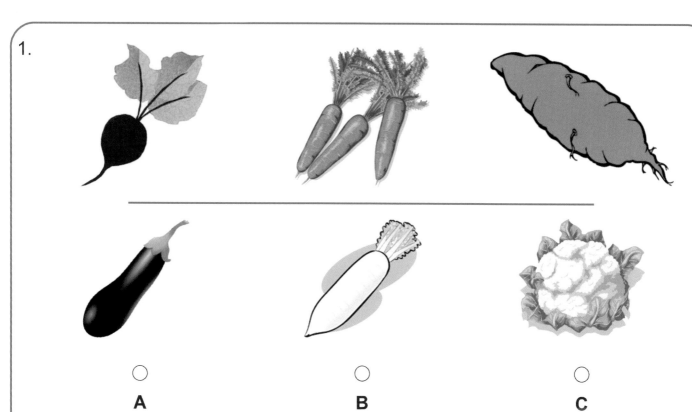

○	○	○
A	**B**	**C**

B is correct. The three pictures in the top row are vegetables that grow below the ground. A is incorrect because it is an eggplant that grows above the ground. C is incorrect because it is a cauliflower that grows above the ground. B is a white radish that grows below the ground, the only correct option. below the ground, the only correct option.

2.

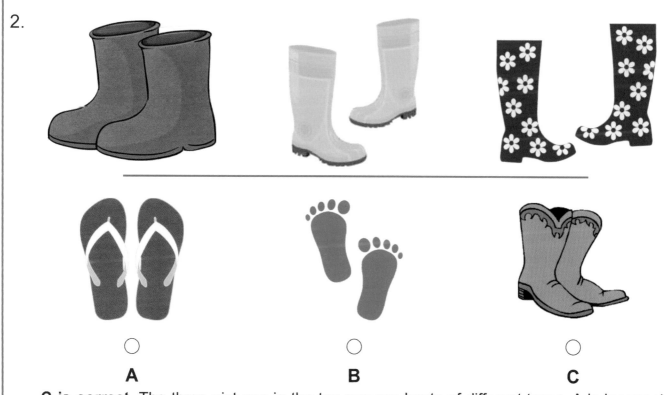

○	○	○
A	**B**	**C**

C is correct. The three pictures in the top row are boots of different types. A is incorrect because it is a slipper. B is incorrect because it is a footprint. C is a boot, the only correct option.

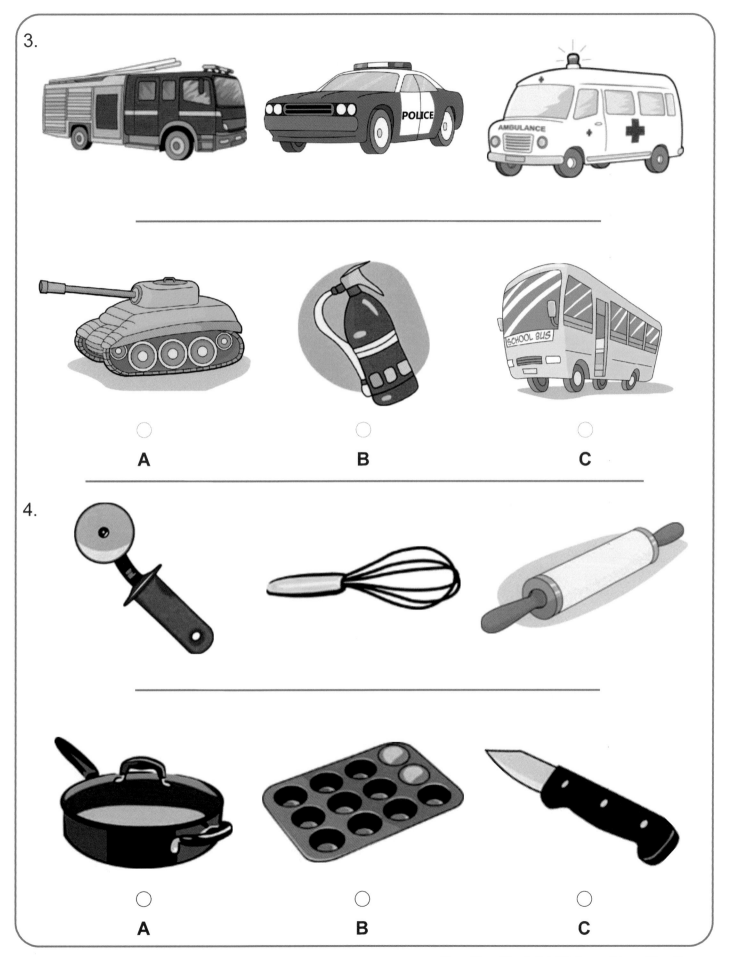

3.

A

B

C

4.

A

B

C

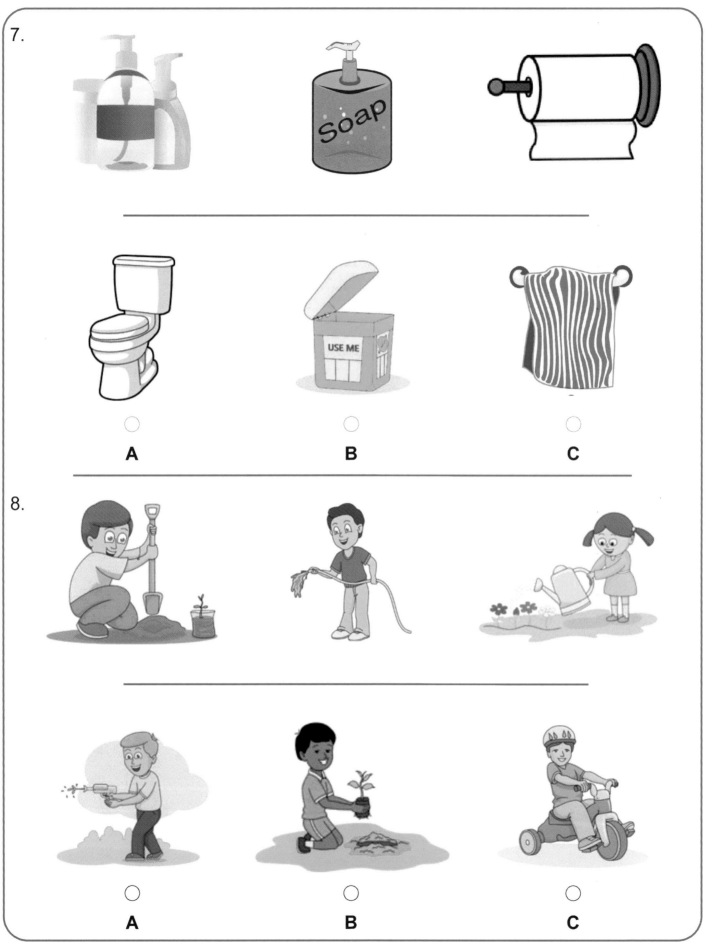

Practice Test 2 | Picture Classification

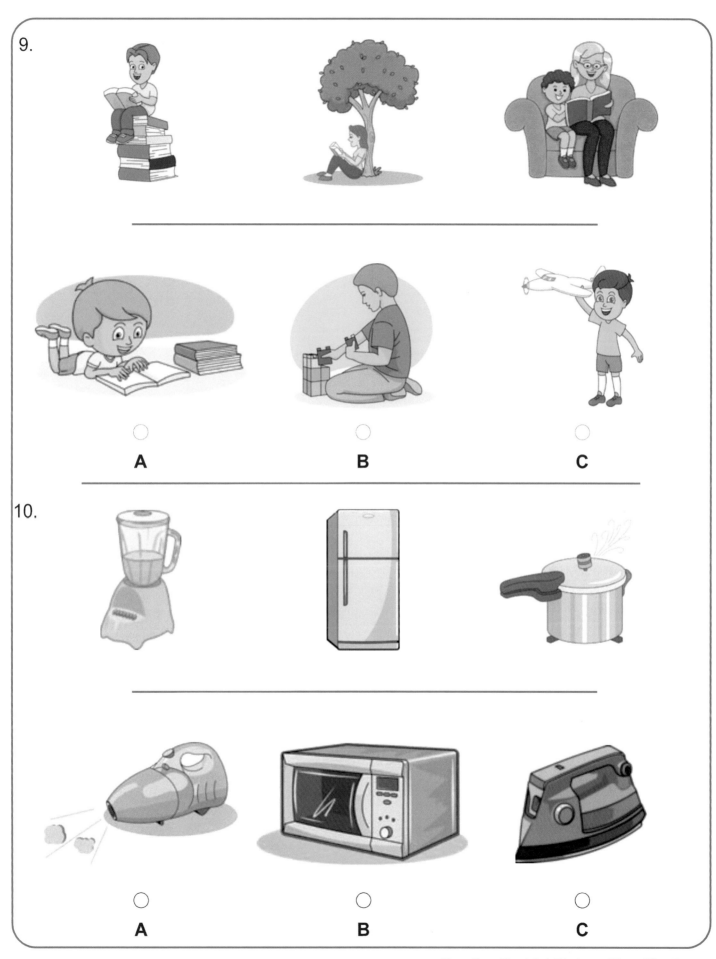

Practice Test 2 | Picture Classification

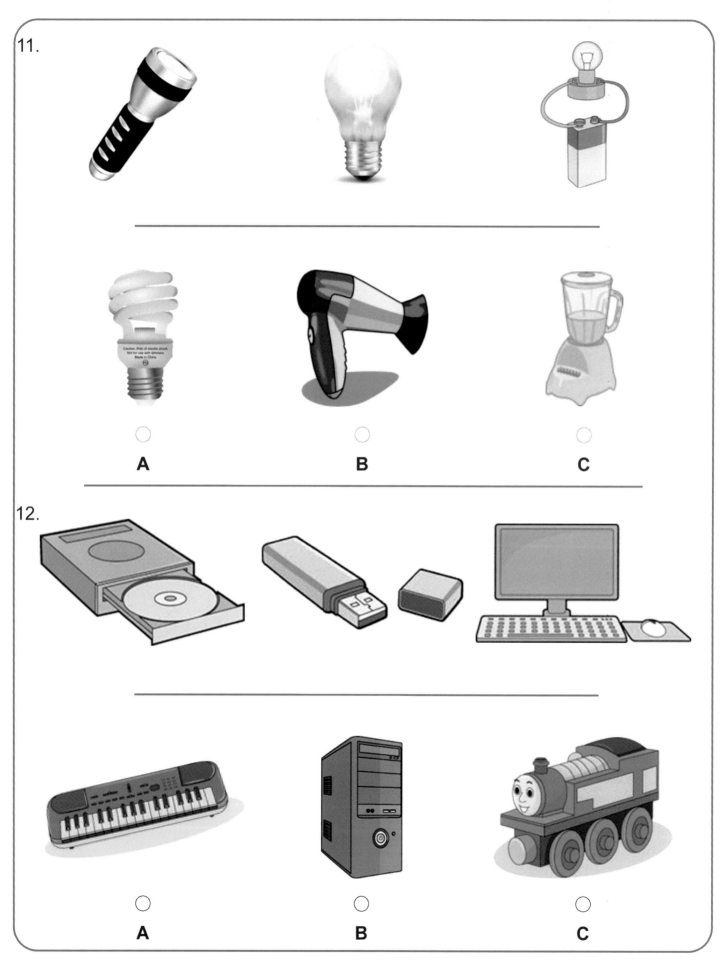

11.

A
B
C

12.

A
B
C

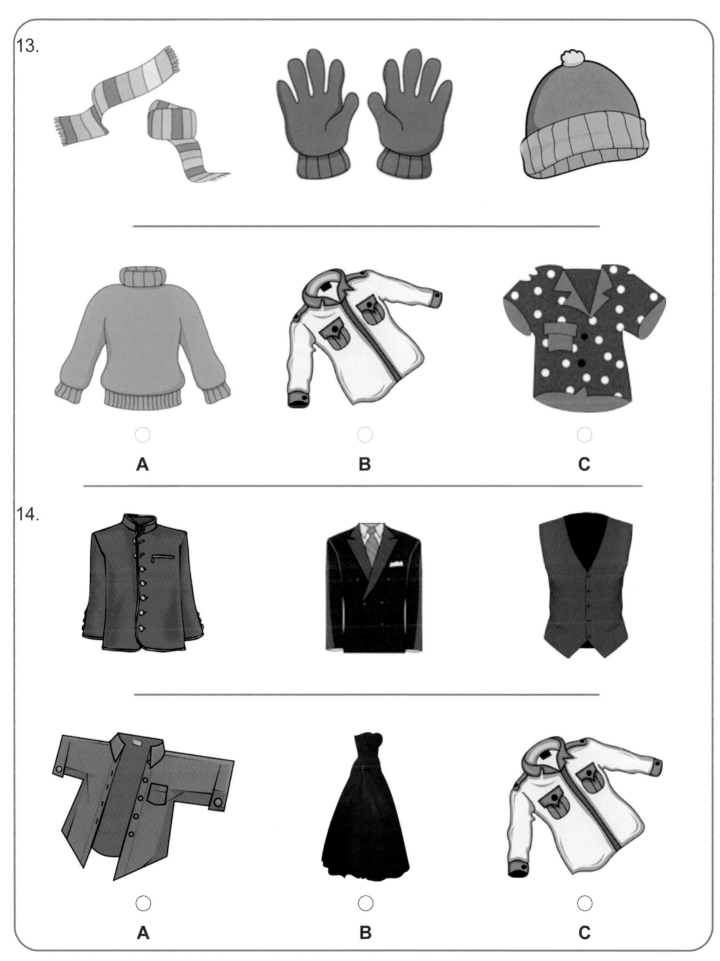

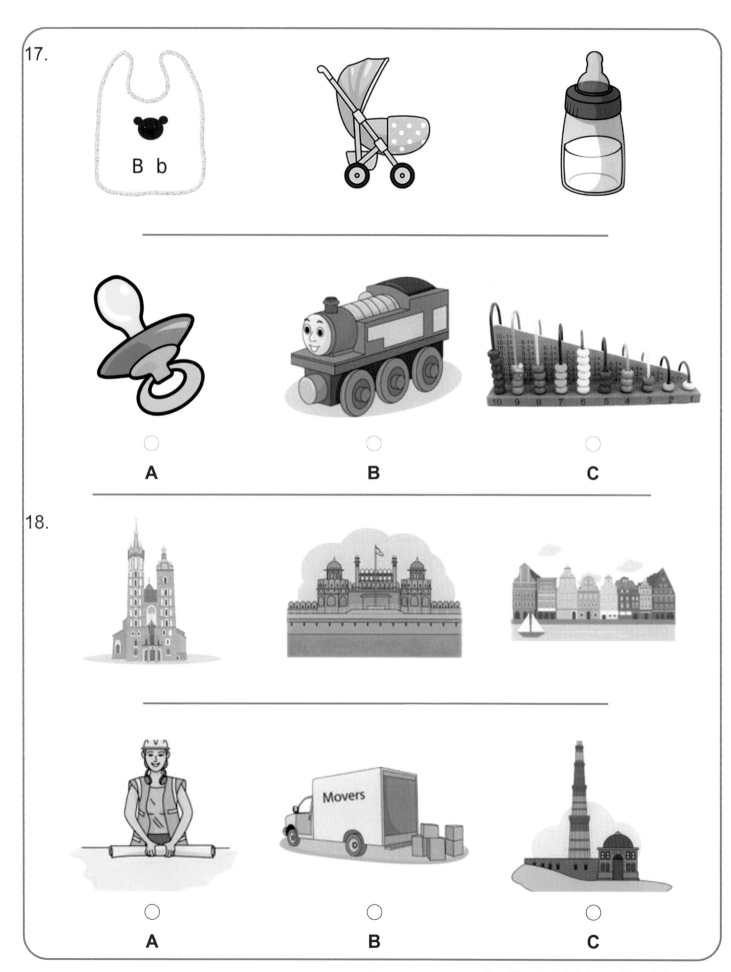

17.

A

B

C

18.

A

B

C

19.

A

B

C

20.

A

B

C

Subset 4: Number Analogies

Instructions:

For each of the questions in this subset, you have to first determine the relationship between the number of objects shown in two pictures in the top row. Next, look at the first picture in the bottom row and from the options provided to you, find the picture that best completes the relationship in the same way as the relationship between the two pictures in the top row. Color the bubble under one option (A,B, or C) that is the best match.

The first two questions are samples and have been solved for you.

1.

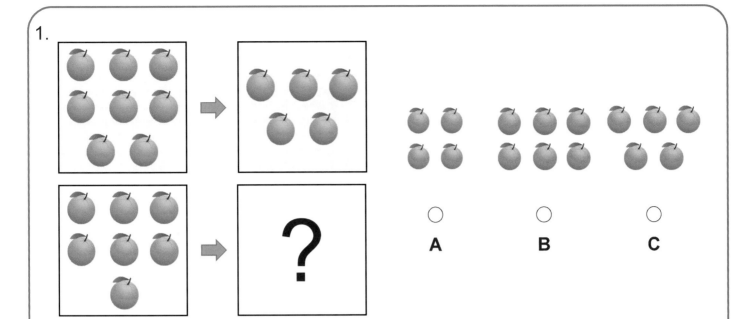

A is correct. In the top row, the first picture shows 8 oranges while the second picture shows 5 oranges, 3 oranges less than the number of oranges in the first picture (8 minus 3 = 5). In the bottom row, the first picture is that of 7 oranges. We need to look for an option which shows 3 oranges less than those shown in first picture (7 minus 3 = 4). Only A shows 4 oranges and is the correct option.

2.

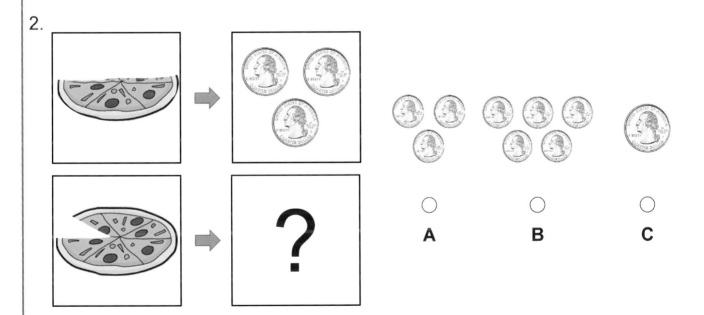

B is correct. In the top row, the first picture shows 3 slices of pizza while the second picture shows 3 quarters, meaning each pizza slice costs one quarter. In the bottom row, the first picture is that of 5 pizza slices. We need to look for an option which shows 5 quarters. Only B shows 5 quarters and is the correct option.

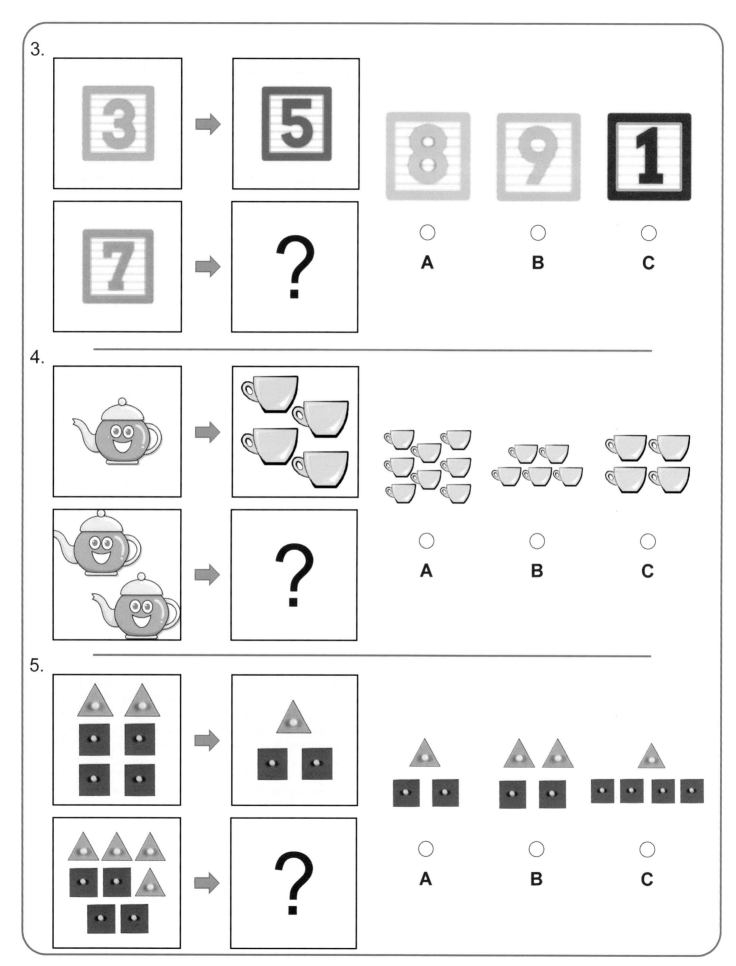

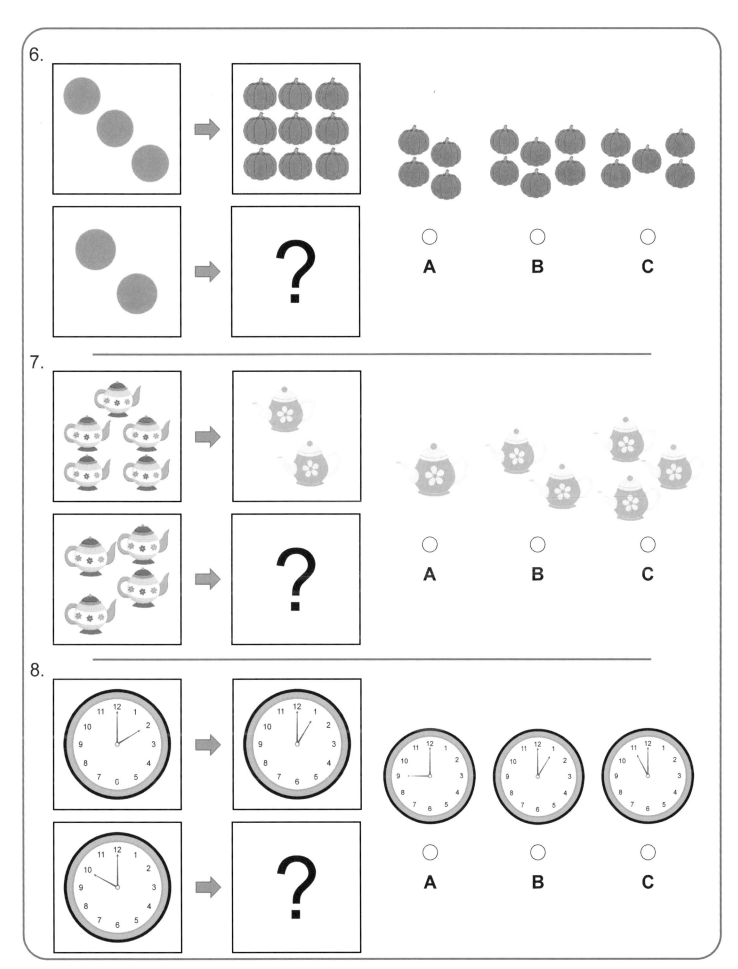

Practice Test 2 | Number Analogies

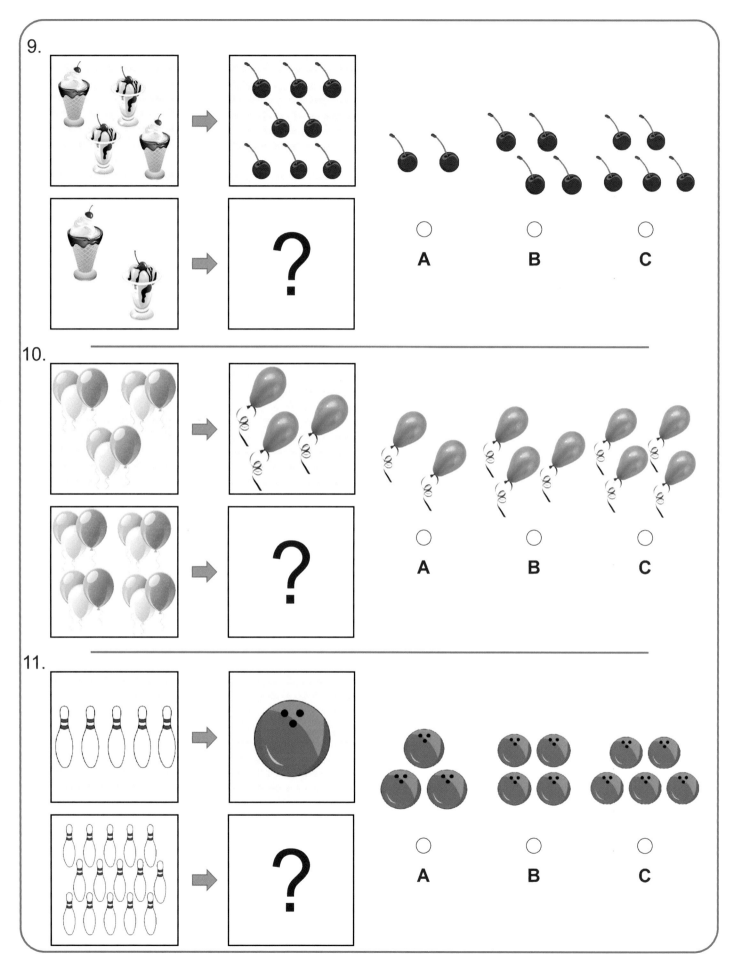

9.

10.

11.

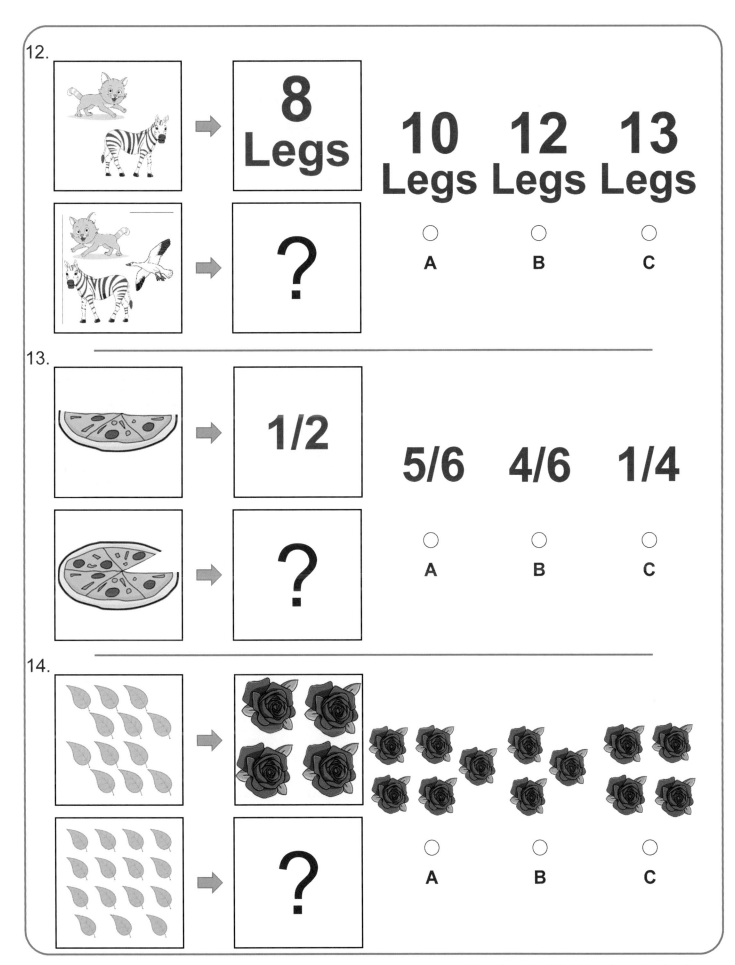

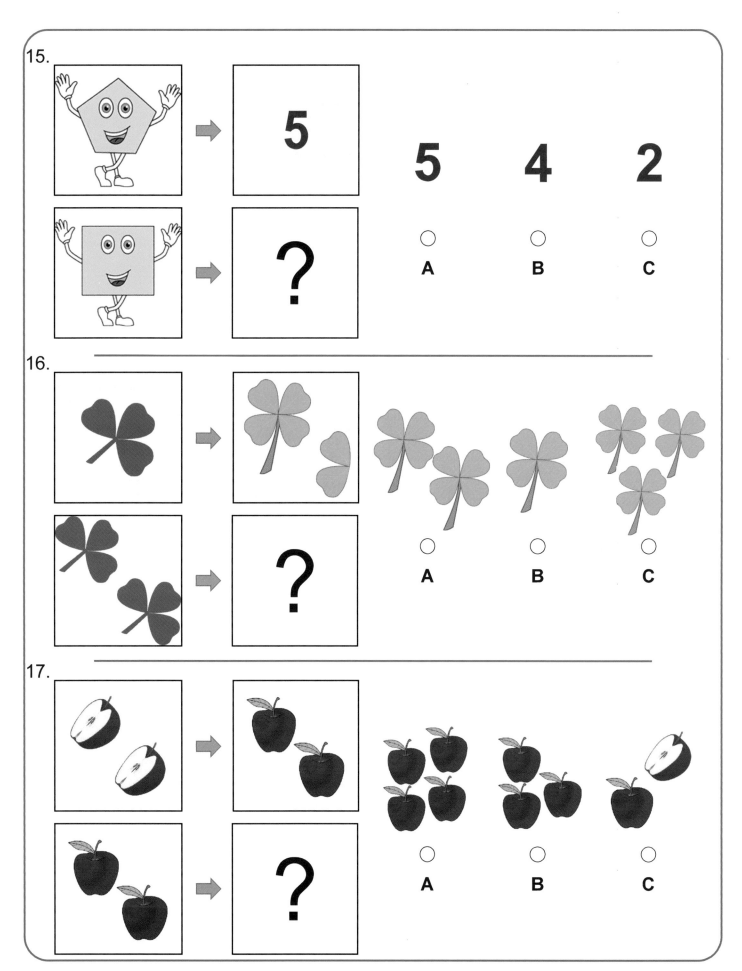

Practice Test 2 | Number Analogies

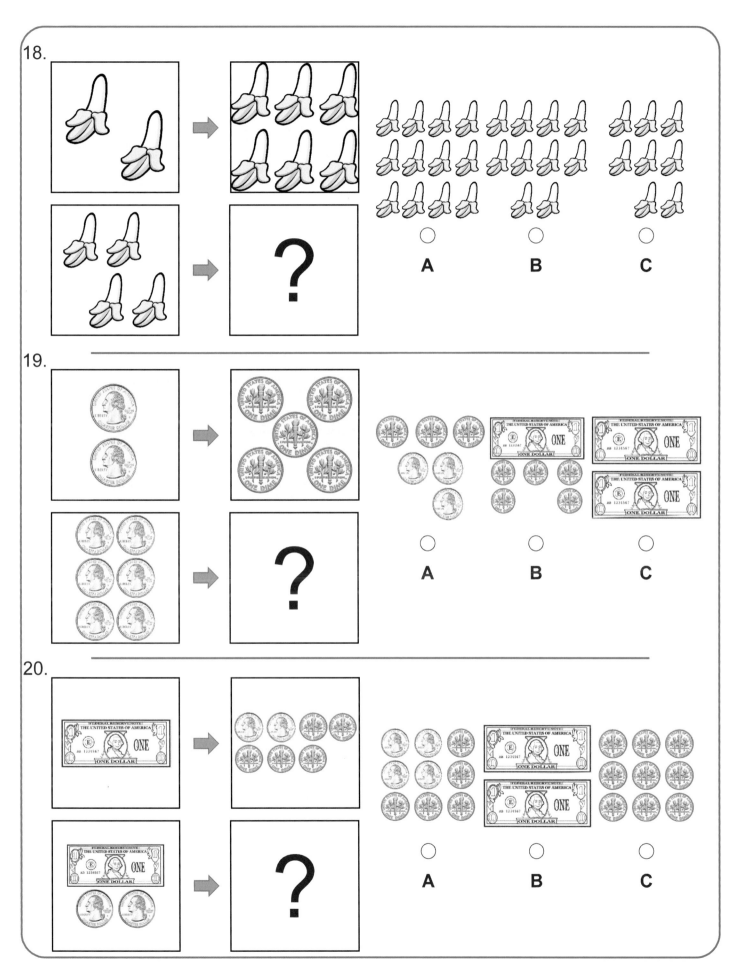

18.

19.

20.

Subset 5: Number Puzzles

Instructions:

For each of the questions in this subset, you will see two trains on either side of the line with cars attached to them. The number of cars attached to each of these trains may not always be the same or there may be no cars attached at all. The cars in each of these trains carry different load.

From the answer options provided to you, you need to find the car that when replaced with the empty car in the question (shown by a "?") balances the load in both the trains. Color the bubble under one option (A,B, or C) that is the best match.

The first two questions are samples and have been solved for you.

1.

A   B   C

A is correct. Your job is to make sure that the trains on either side carry the same load. The picture of the train on the left shows there are 4 circles in the green car and 6 circles in the pink car. The total of the green and pink cars is 10 (4+6). Now look at the picture of the train on the right. It shows there are 5 circles in the green car. You need 5 more circles in the pink car to make the total equal to 10. Only A has 5 circles and is the correct answer.

2.

A   B   C

C is correct. Your job is to make sure that the trains on either side carry the same load. The picture of the train on the left shows there are 10 hexagons in the yellow car. Now look at the picture of the train on the right. It shows there are 4 hexagons in the pink car and 5 hexagons in the yellow car. You need 1 more hexagon in the green car to make the total equal to 10. Only C has 1 hexagon and is the correct answer.

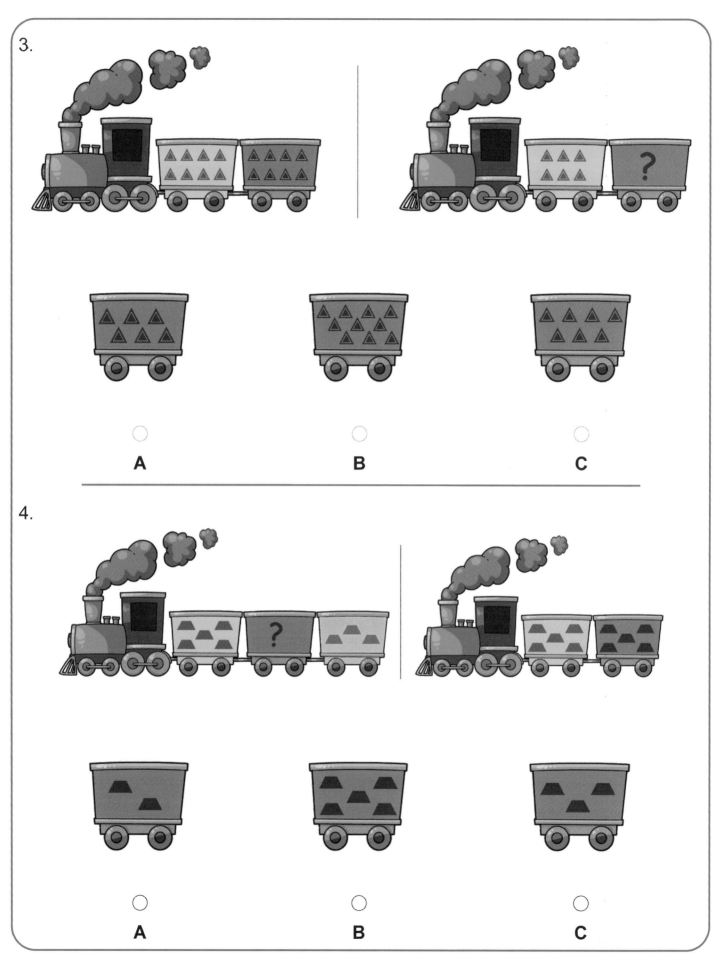

3.

A

B

C

4.

A

B

C

Practice Test 2 | Number Puzzles

5.

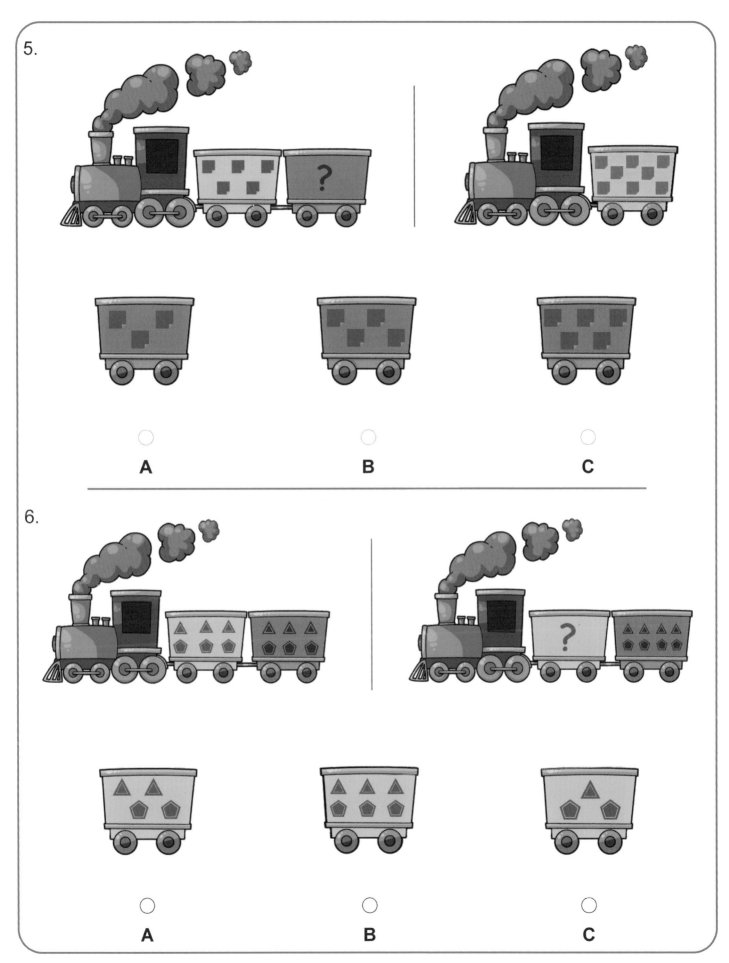

A   B   C

6.

A   B   C

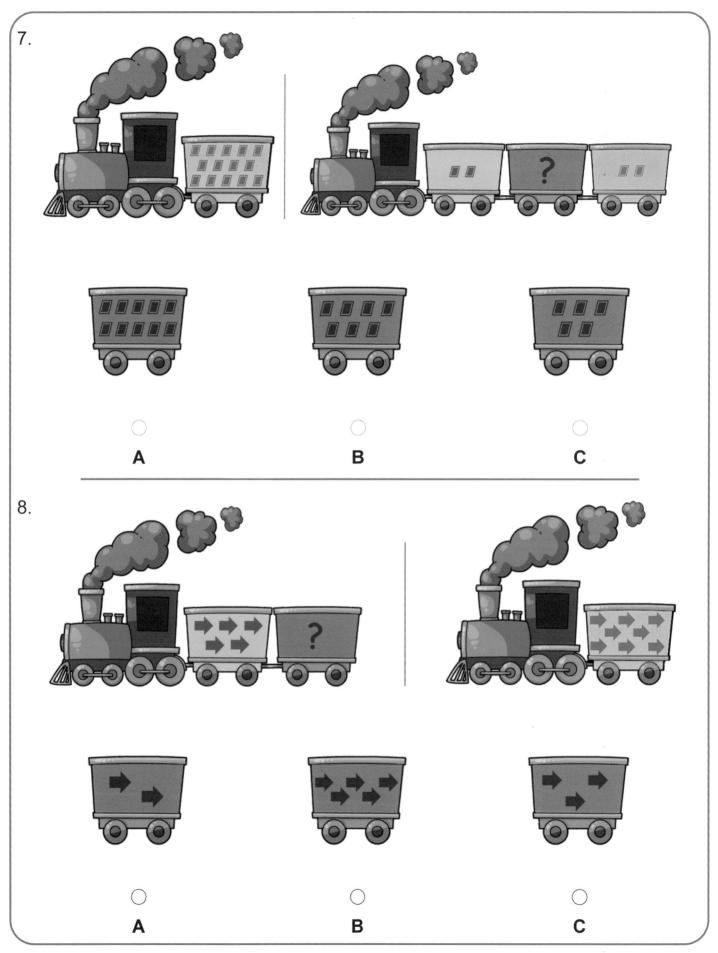

7.

A   B   C

8.

A   B   C

9.

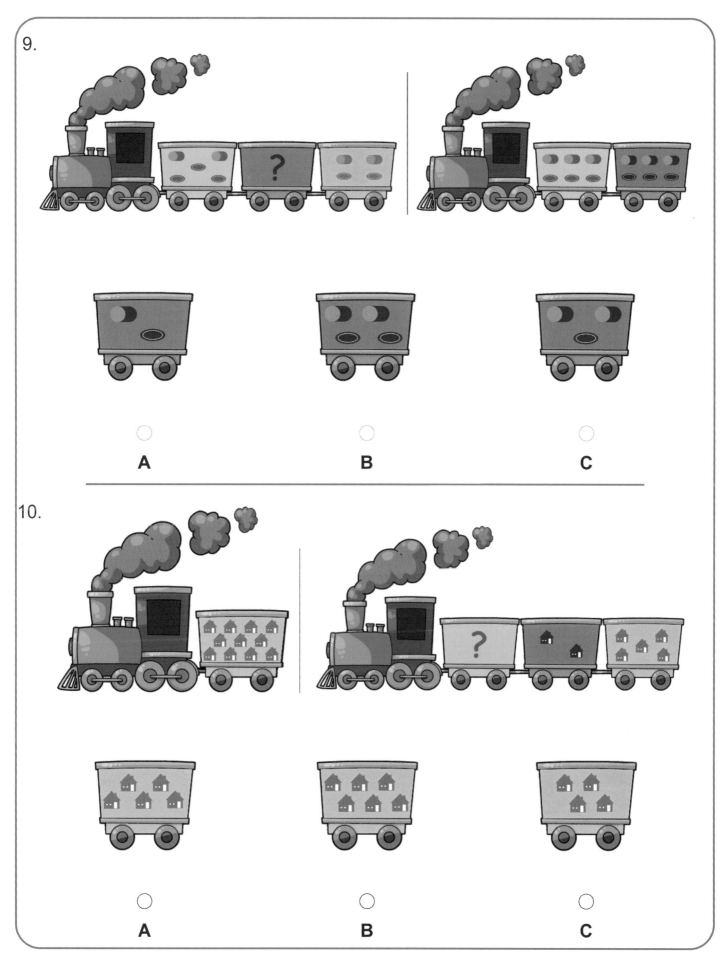

A

B

C

10.

A

B

C

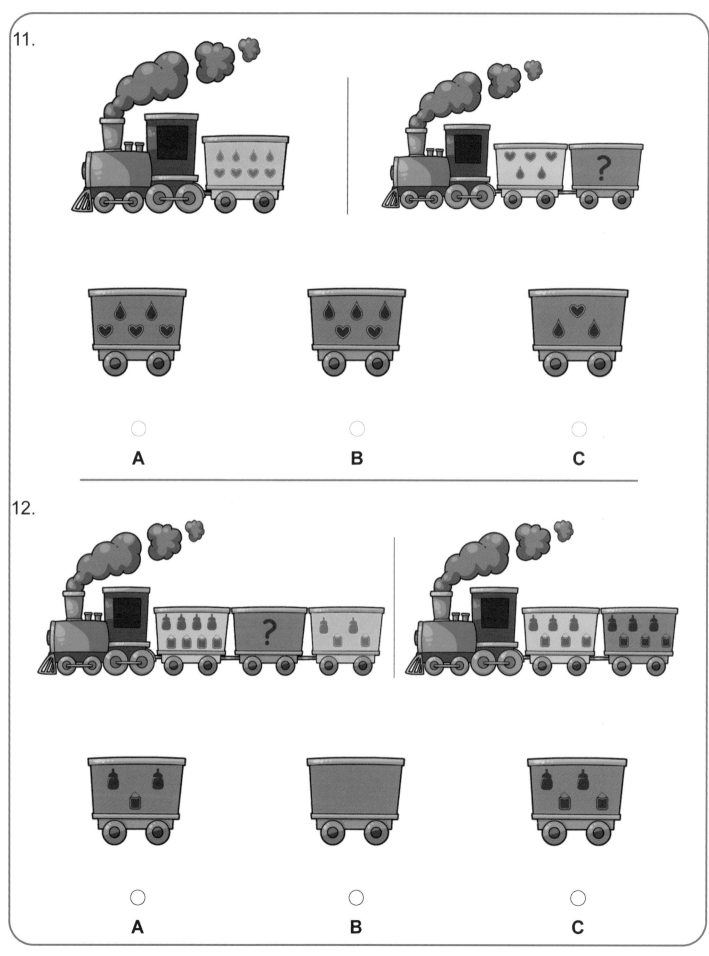

11.

A

B

C

12.

A

B

C

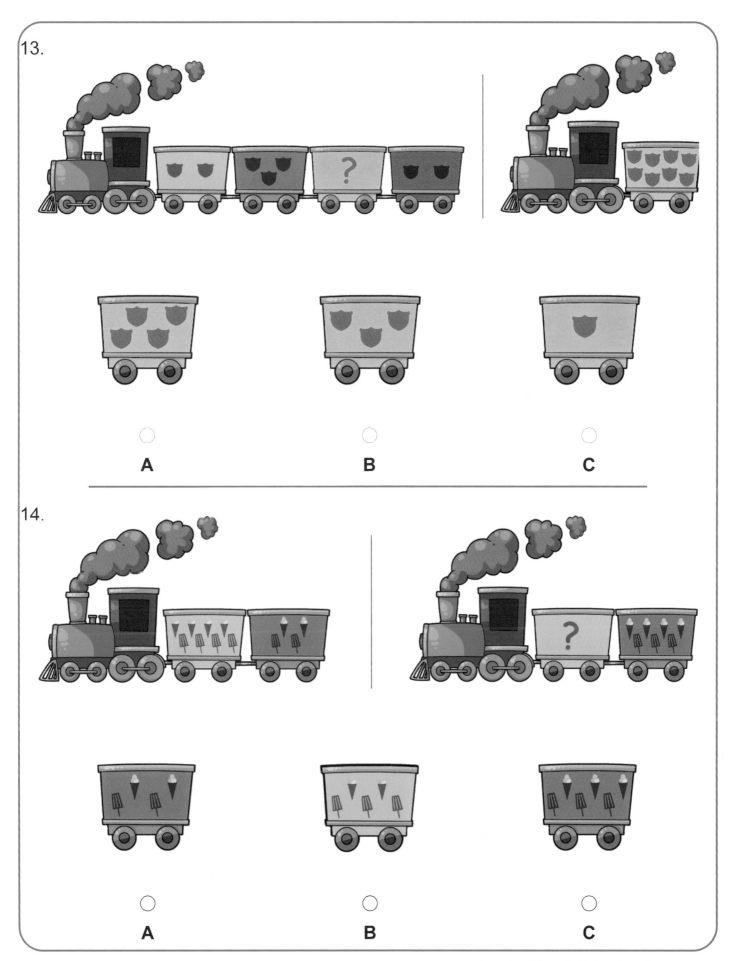

13.

A   B   C

14.

A   B   C

151   Practice Test 2 | Number Puzzles

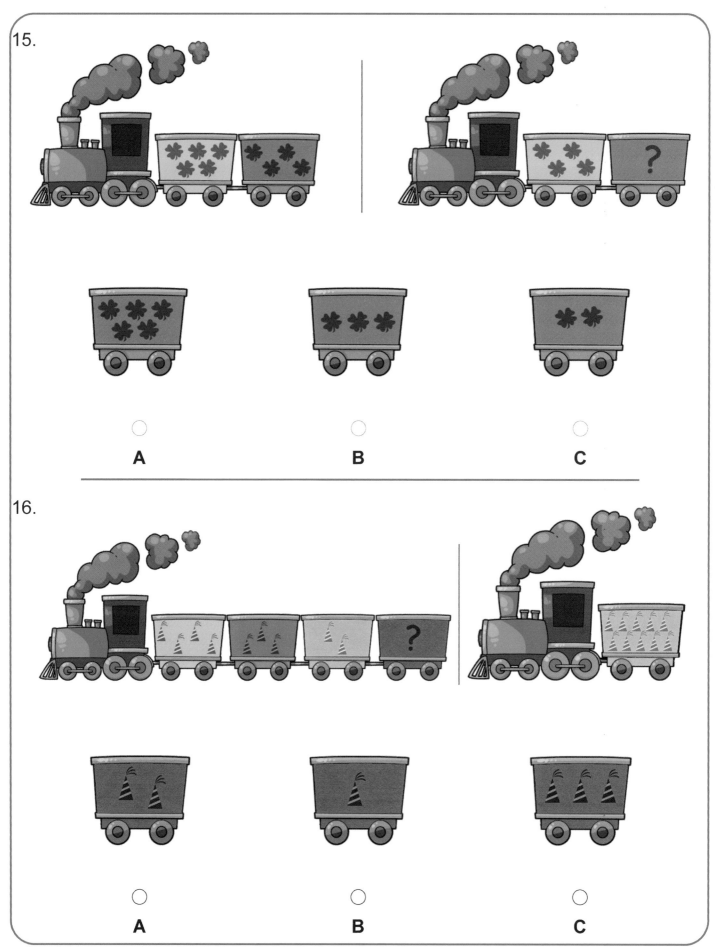

15.

A

B

C

16.

A

B

C

Subset 6: Number Series

Instructions:

For each of the questions in this subset, you will see an abacus with some pattern represented by the number of beads in the rods. From the answer options provided to you, you need to find the rod with beads that when replaced with the empty rod in the abacus (shown by a "?") completes the pattern. Color the bubble under one option (A,B, or C) that is the best match.

The first two questions are samples and have been solved for you.

1.

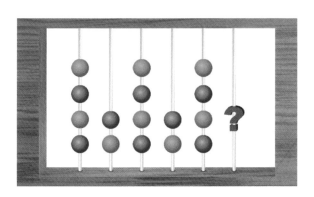   

A   B   C

B is correct. Your job is to find the option that has the rod with beads that best fit in the missing rod in the abacus in question (shown by a "?"). The pattern (from left to right) in the abacus shows rods with beads in alternate equal numbers where the odd numbered rods (1,3,5) carry 4 beads and the even numbered rods (2,4,..) carry 2 beads. The missing rod in question is even numbered (6). Only B completes this pattern and is the correct answer.

2.

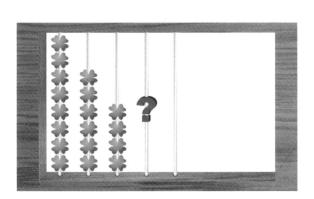   

A   B   C

C is correct. Your job is to find the option that has the rod with beads that best fit in the missing rod in the abacus in question (shown by a "?"). The pattern (from left to right) in the abacus shows rods with beads in descending order of numbers where each rod after the first carries 2 beads less than the rod on its left. Only C completes this pattern and is the correct answer.

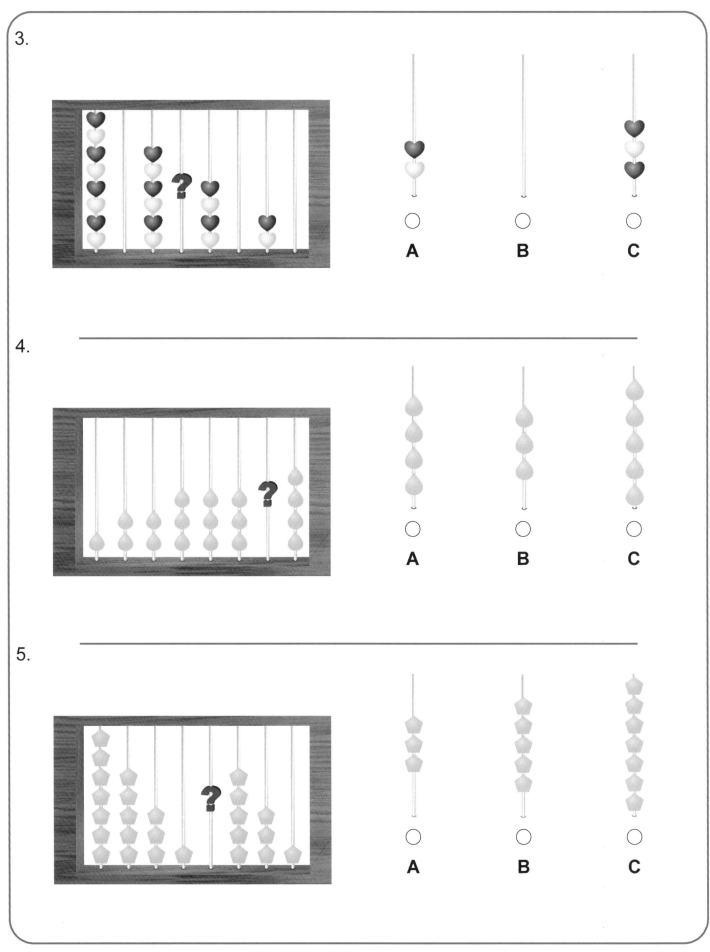

3.

4.

5.

6.

7.

8.

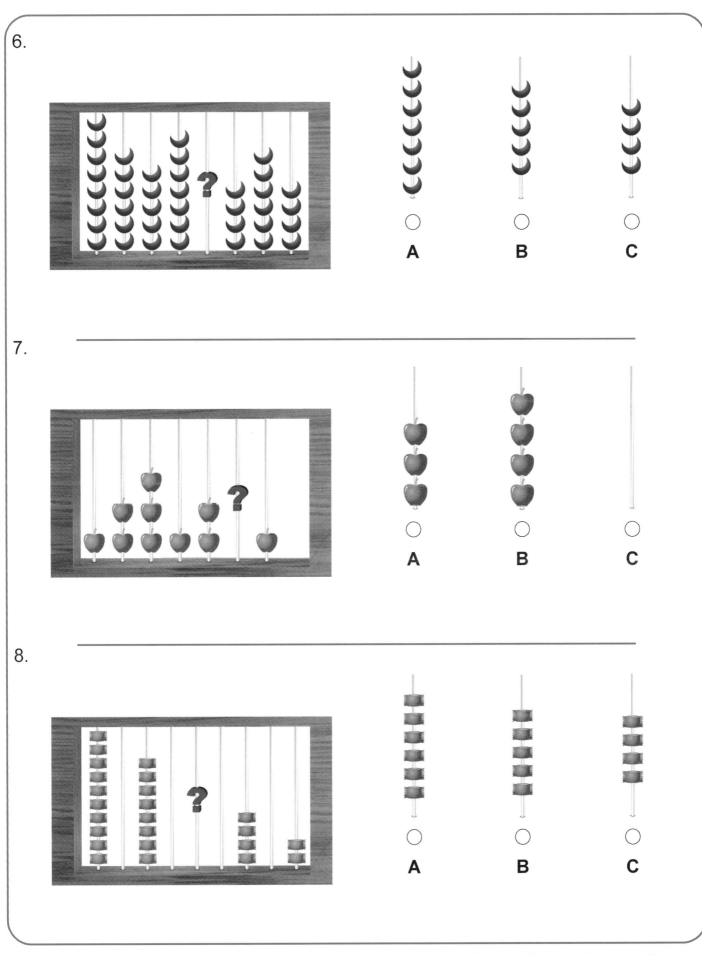

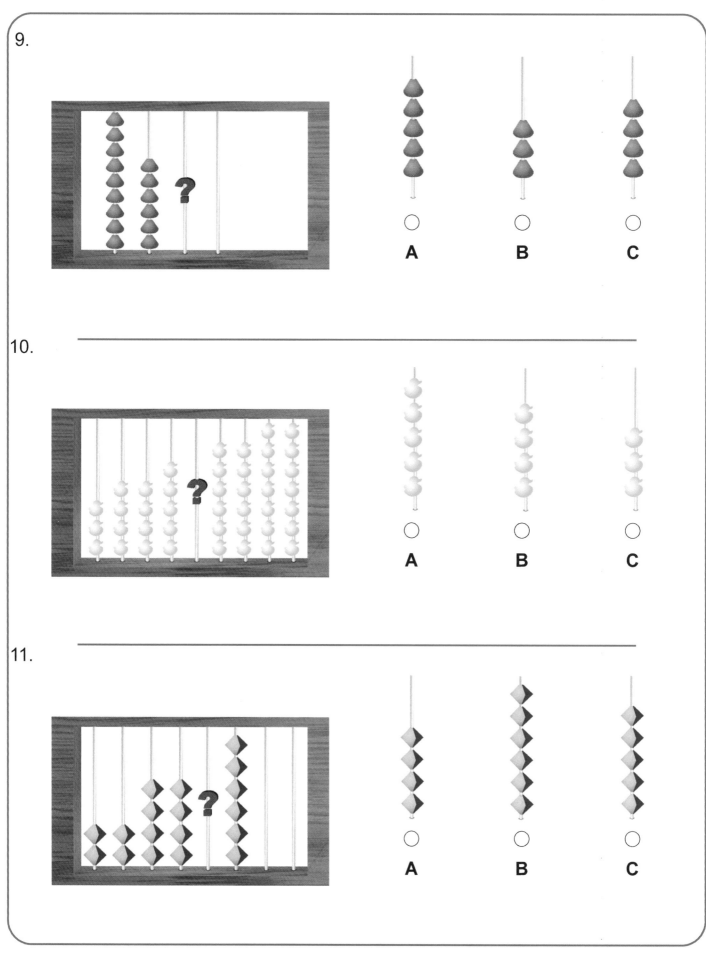

12.

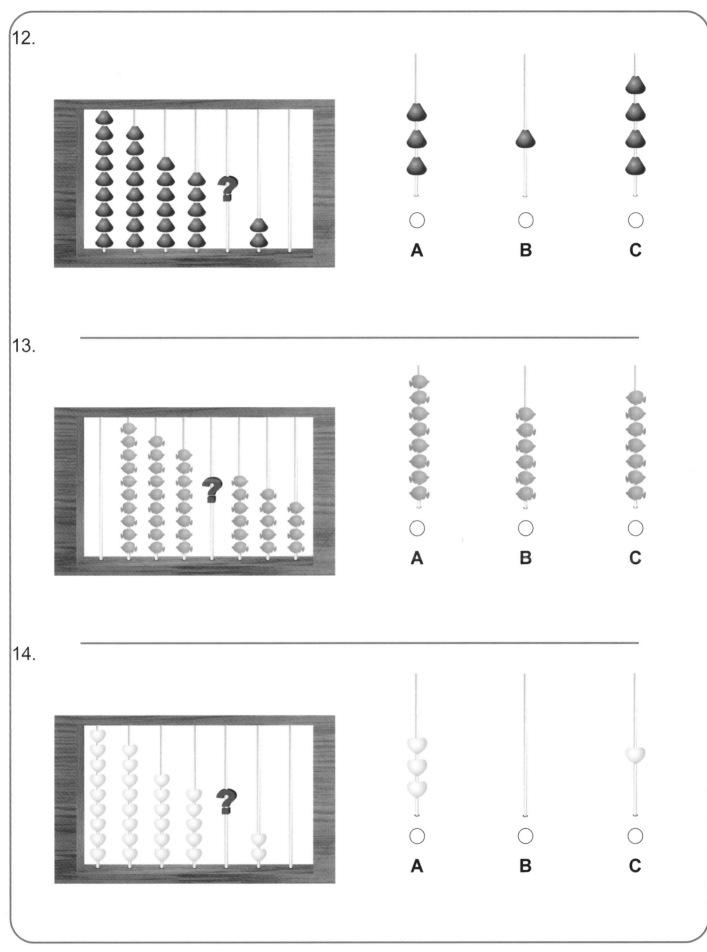

13.

14.

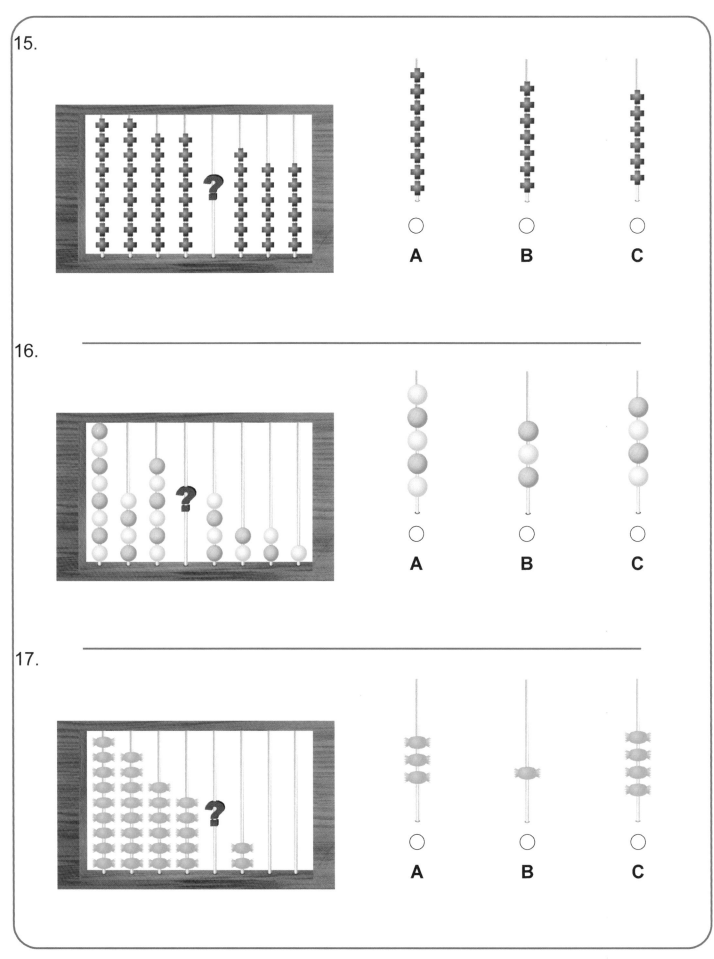

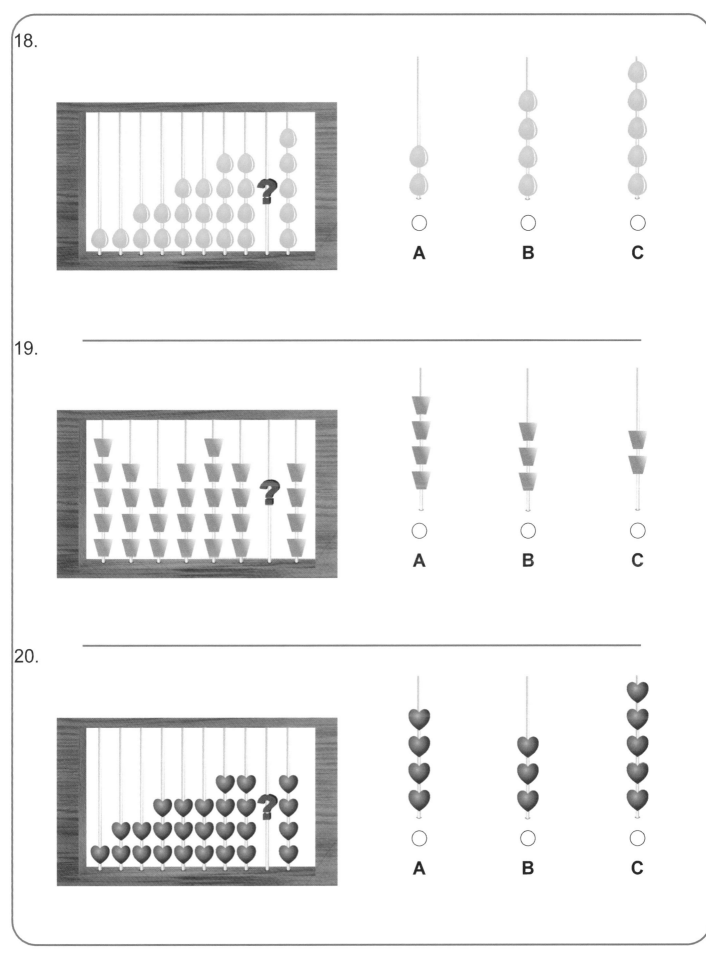

18.

A   B   C

19.

A   B   C

20.

A   B   C

Subset 7: Figure Matrices

Instructions:

For each of the questions in this subset, you have to first determine the relationship between the two figures in the top row. Next, look at the first figure in the bottom row and from the options provided to you, find the figure that best completes the relationship in the same way as the relationship between the two figures in the top row. Color the bubble under one option (A,B, or C) that is the best match.

The first two questions are samples and have been solved for you.

1.

B is correct. Your job is to find the option that best fits the empty box in the bottom row (shown by a "?"). The two pictures in the top row show a relationship – the picture to the right is a mirror image of the picture to the left. The bottom row should exhibit the same relationship. Only B is the mirror image of the picture on the left side in the bottom row and is the correct answer.

2.

B is correct. Your job is to find the option that best fits the empty box in the bottom row (shown by a "?"). The two pictures in the top row show a relationship – the picture to the right is an inverted image of the picture to the left and has one object less compared to the picture on the left. The bottom row should exhibit the same relationship. Only B completes the relationship and is the correct answer.

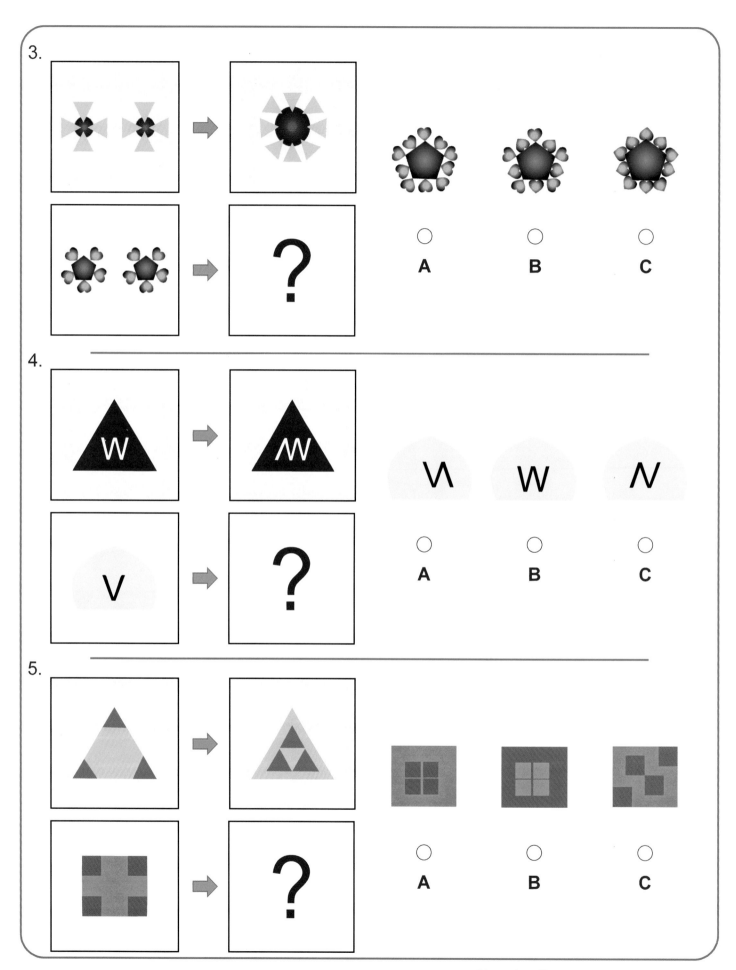

Practice Test 2 | Figure Matrices

6.

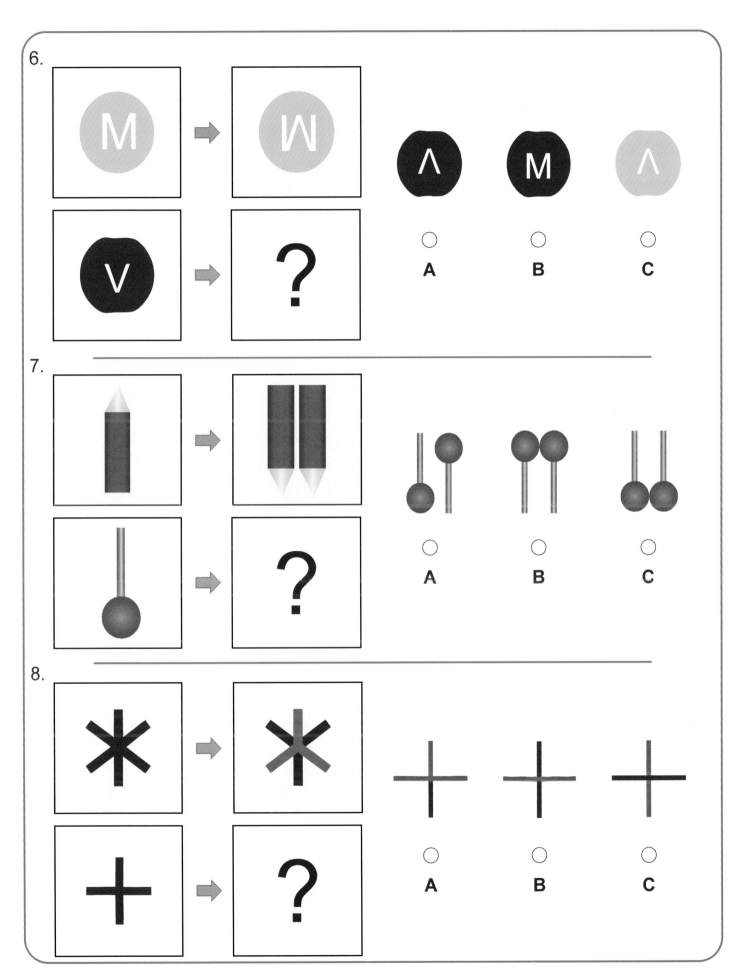

7.

8.

167   Practice Test 2 | Figure Matrices

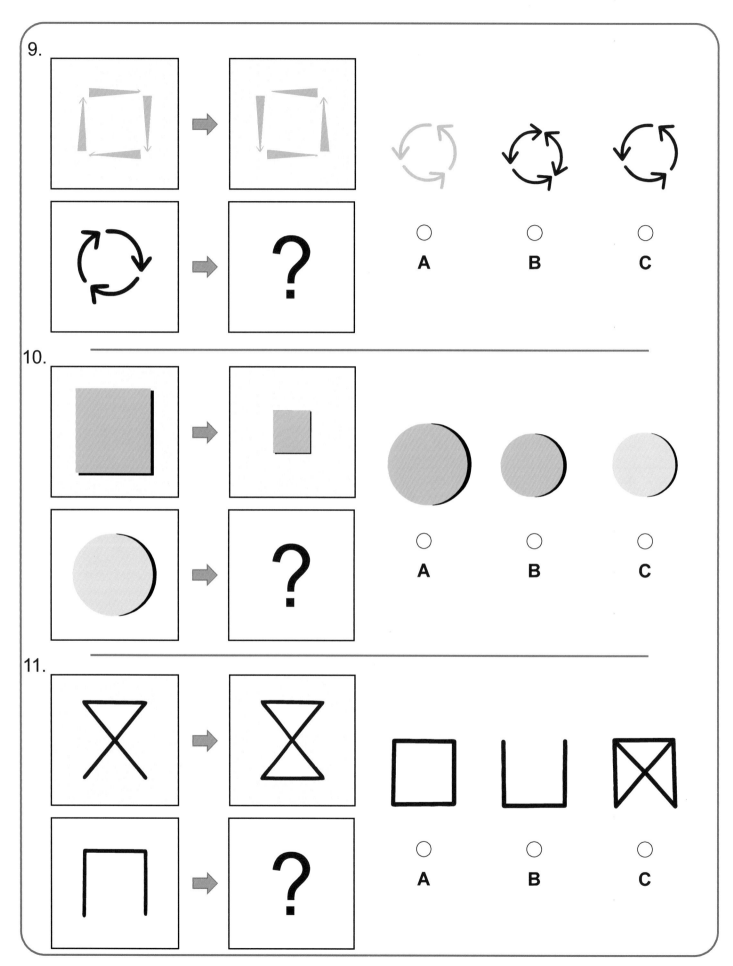

9.

10.

11.

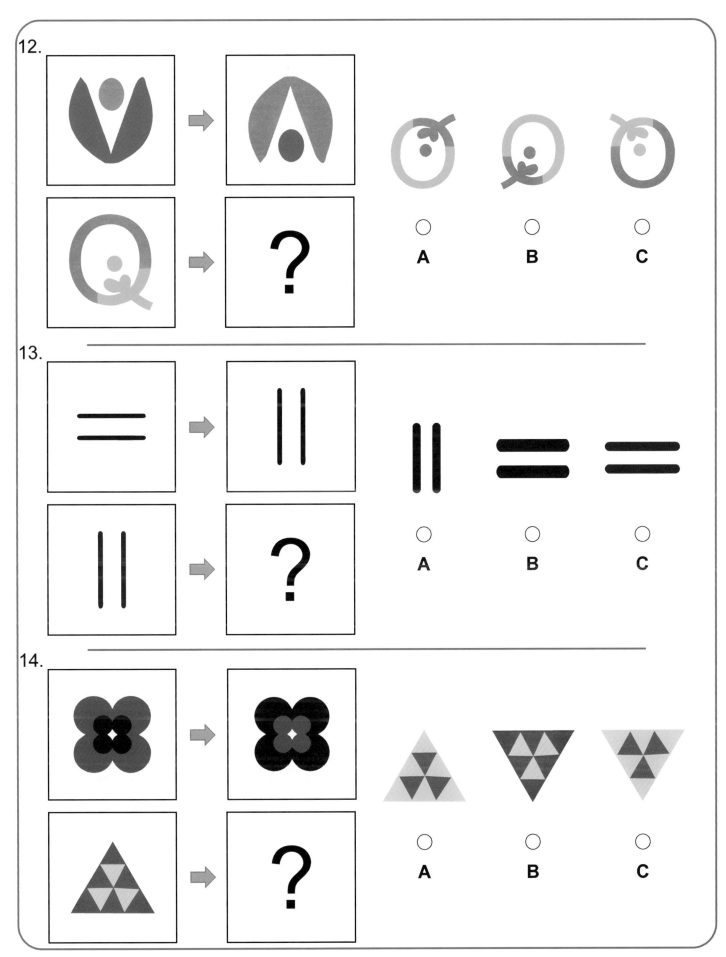

Practice Test 2 | Figure Matrices

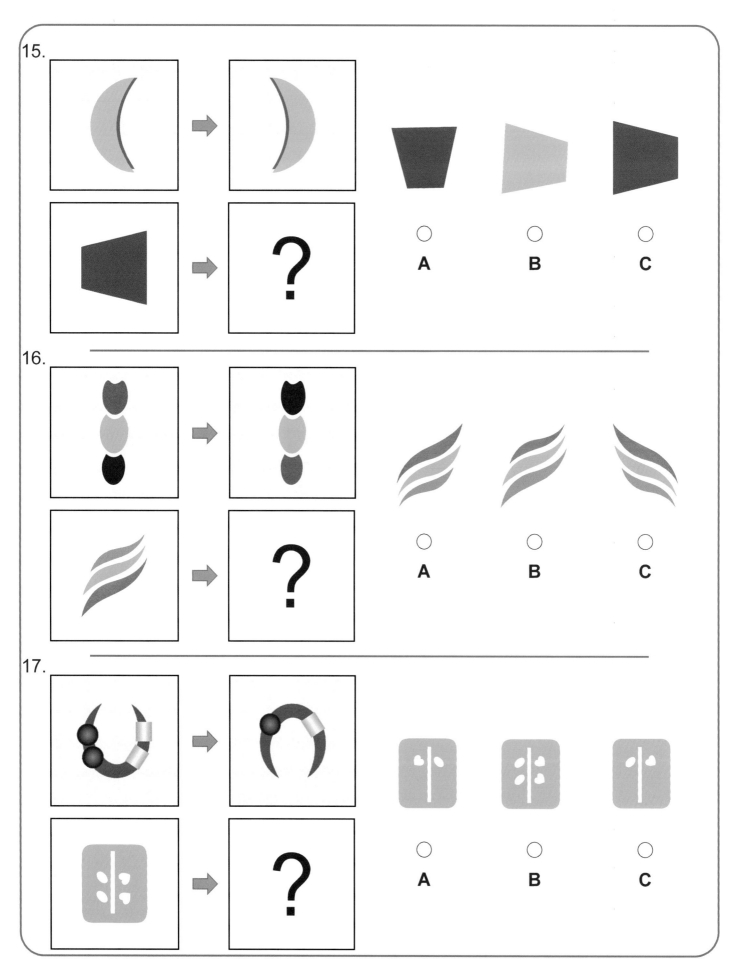

15.

16.

17.

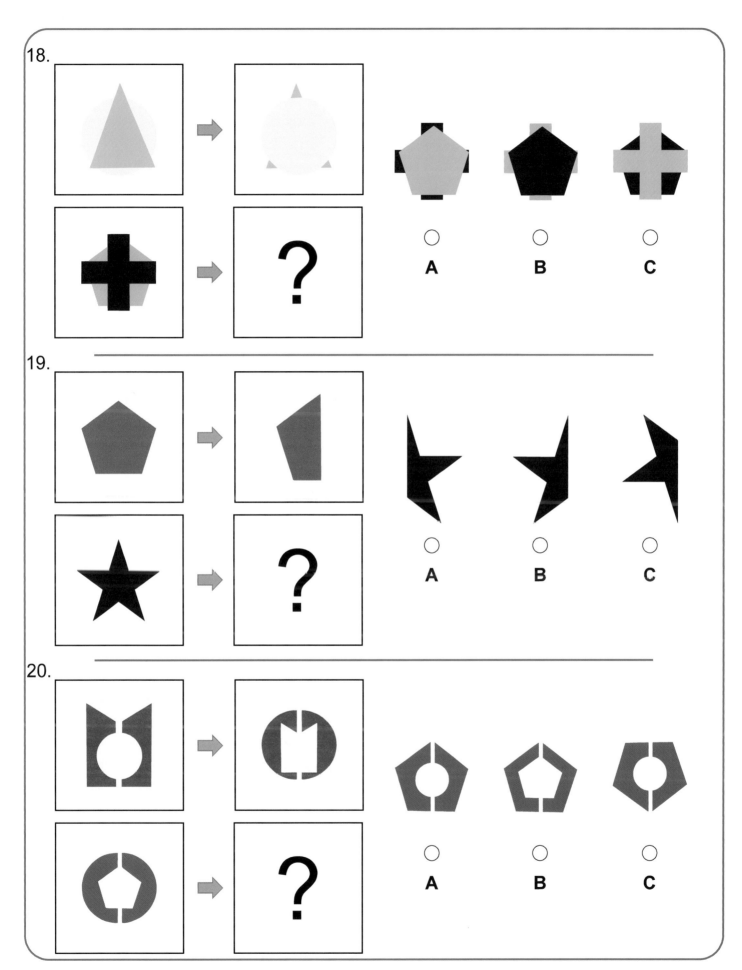

Subset 8: Paper Folding

Instructions:

For each of the questions in this subset, you will see a piece of paper that has been folded along a line shown and then has been either cut with a pair of scissors or has holes punched through it. From the answer options provided to you, you need to find the option that best shows how the paper will look when it is unfolded. Color the bubble under one option (A,B, or C) that is the best match.

The first two questions are samples and have been solved for you.

1.

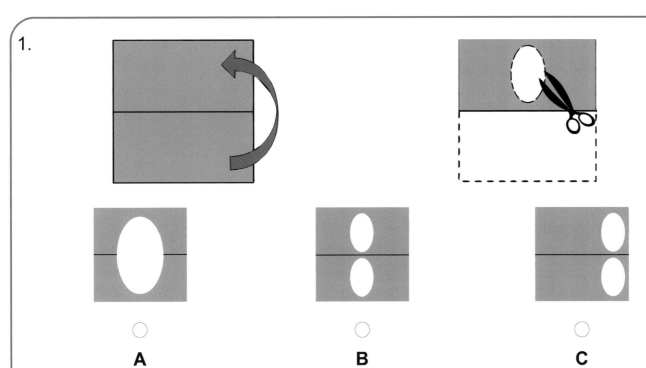

A   B   C

B is correct. In the question, the flow of pictures from left to right shows you how a piece of paper is folded along a solid line and then a hole is punched through it. Your job is to find the option that shows how the paper will look when it is unfolded. Only B shows accurately how the unfolded paper will look and is the correct answer.

2.

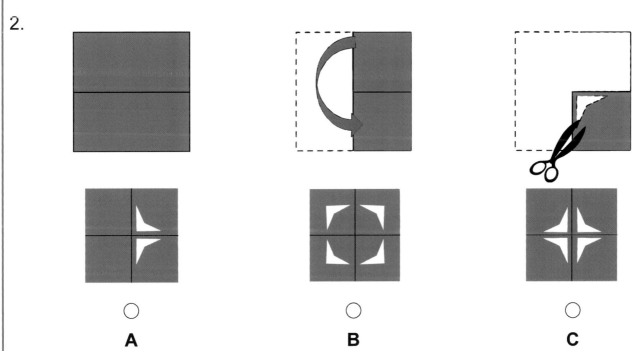

A   B   C

C is correct. In the question, the flow of pictures from left to right shows you how a piece of paper is folded along a solid line and then cut with a pair of scissors. Your job is to find the option that shows how the paper will look when it is unfolded. Only C shows accurately how the unfolded paper will look and is the correct answer.

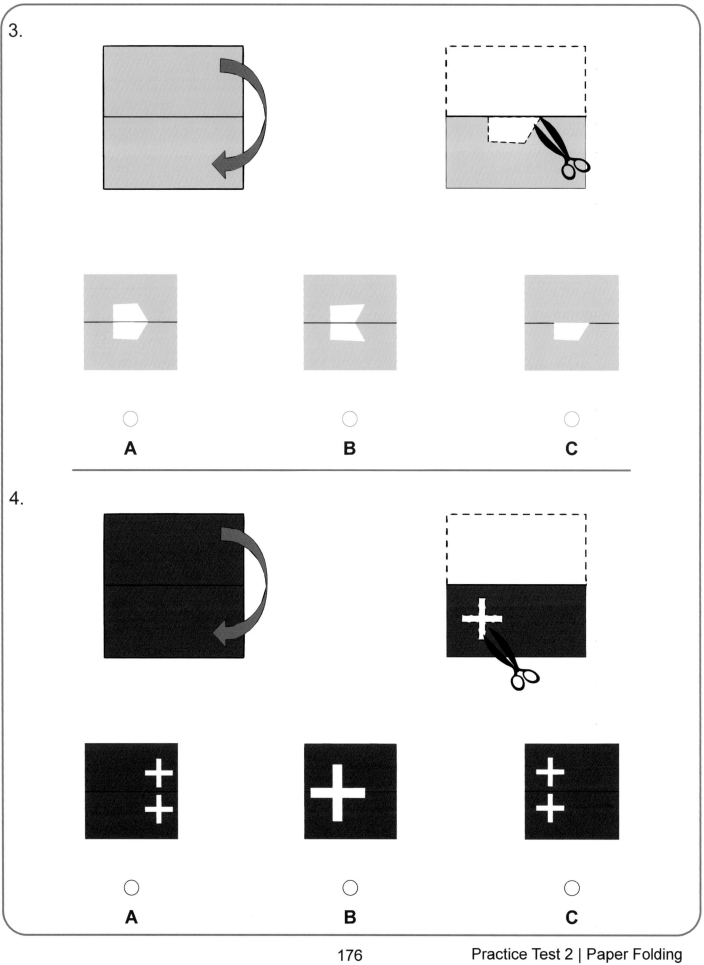

Practice Test 2 | Paper Folding

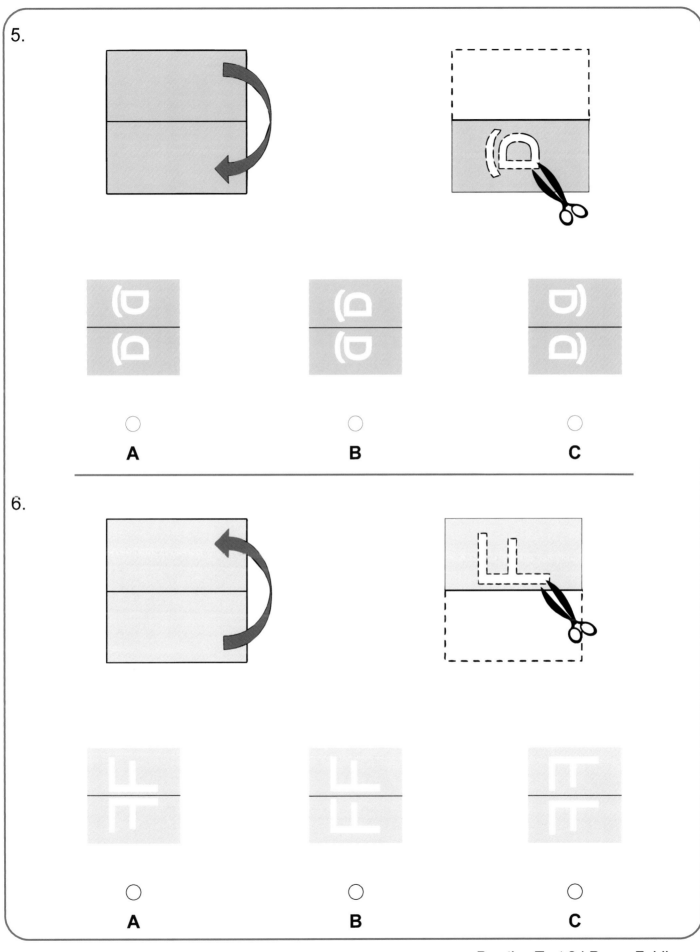

5.

A

B

C

6.

A

B

C

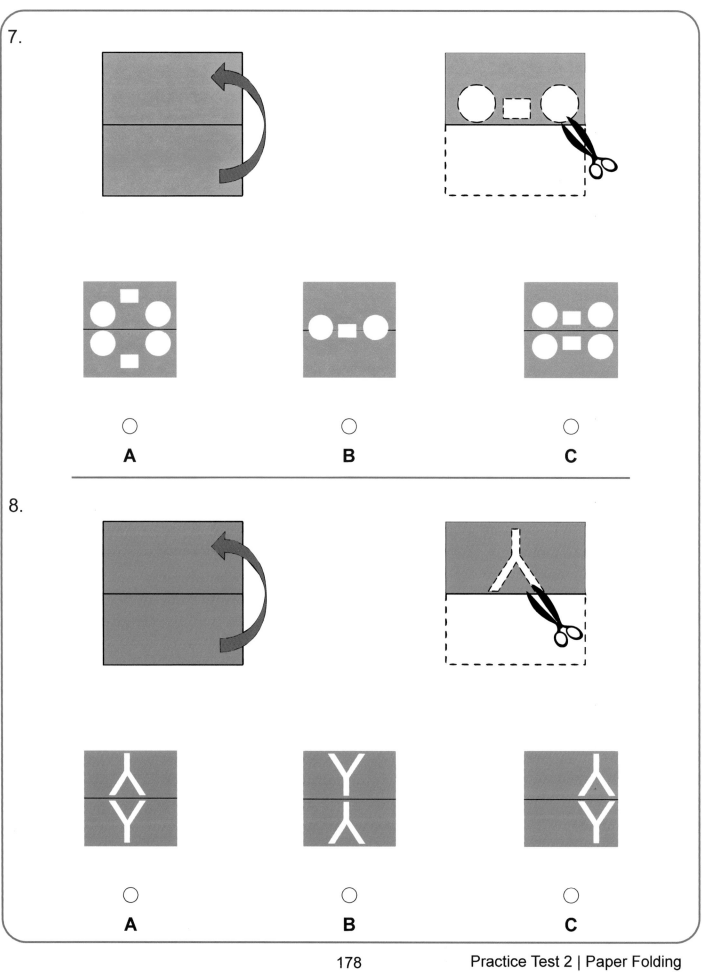

9.

○   ○   ○

A   **B**   **C**

10.

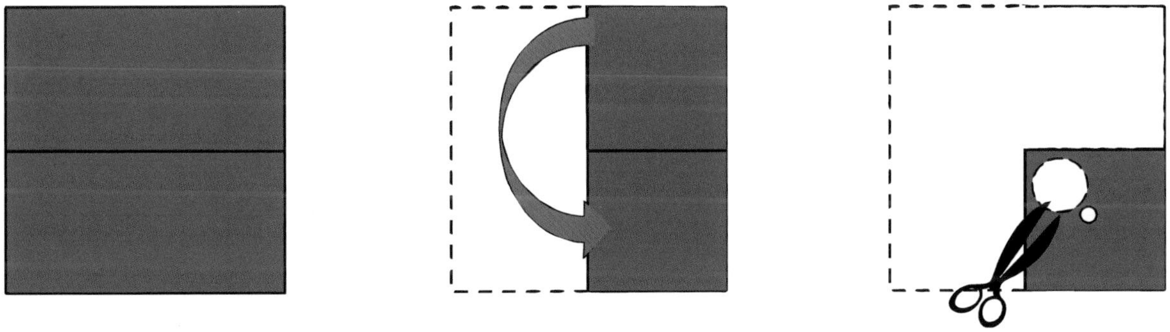

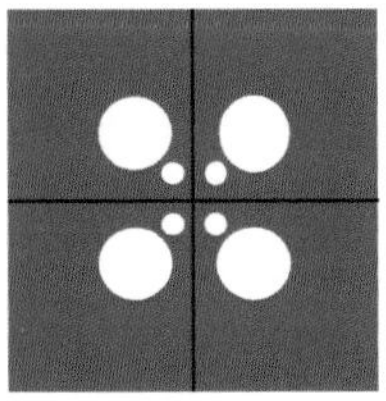

○   ○   ○

A   **B**   **C**

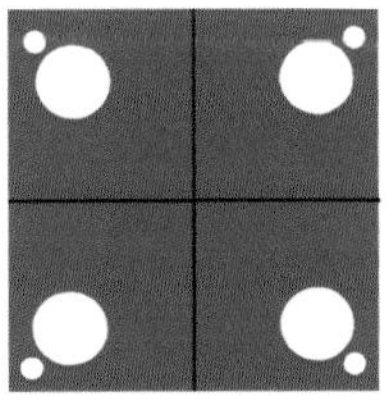

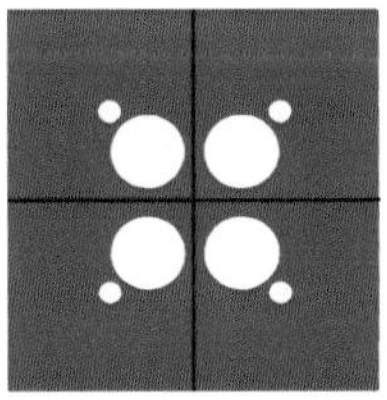

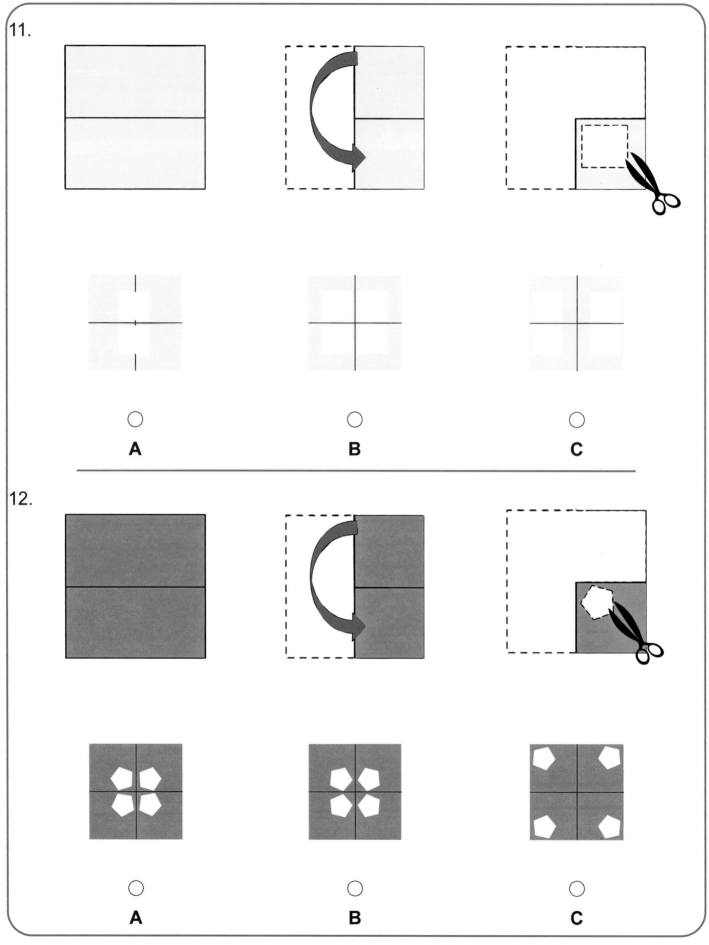

11.

A   B   C

12.

A   B   C

Practice Test 2 | Paper Folding

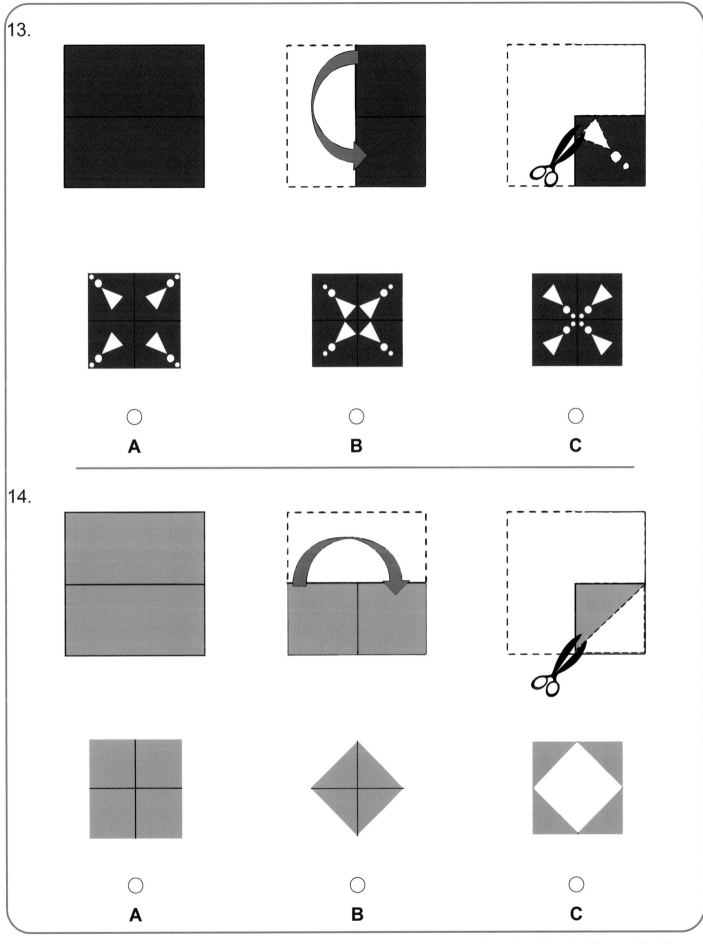

13.

A B C

14.

A B C

Practice Test 2 | Paper Folding

15.

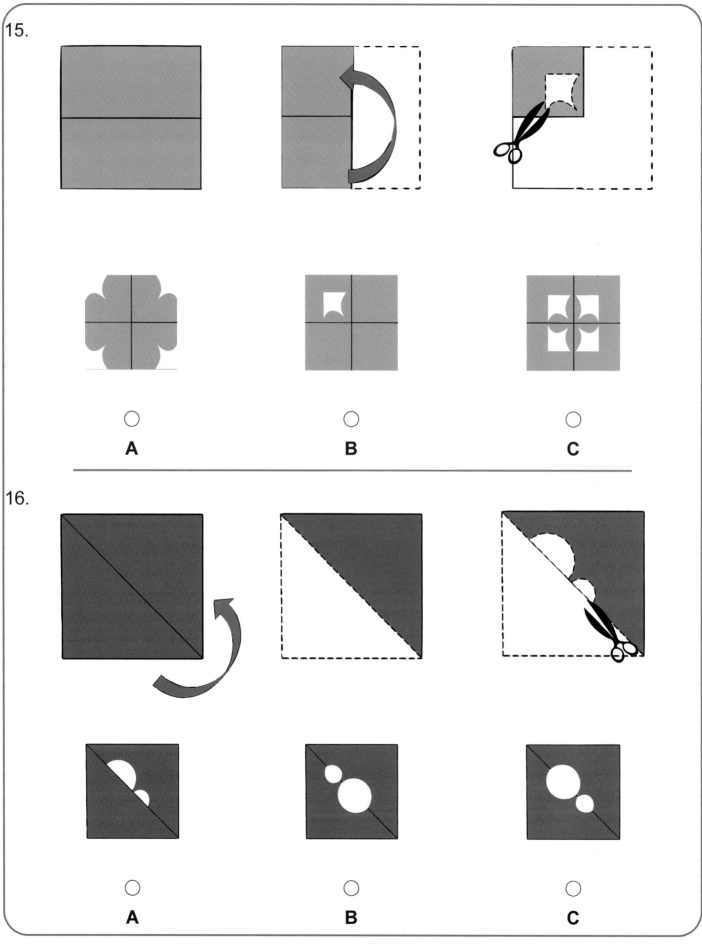

A   B   C

16.

A   B   C

Subset 9: Figure Classification

Instructions:

For each of the questions in this subset, first look at the three figures on the left side of the line and determine how they are similar. Next, look at the figures on the right side of the line and color the bubble under one option (A,B, or C) that is the best match.

The first two questions are samples and have been solved for you.

1.

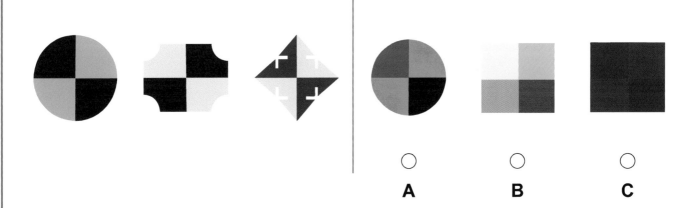

	A	B	C

C is correct. Your job is to find the option with the picture that most closely resembles the three pictures on the left. All the pictures on the left have four equal parts with the opposite parts in same color. Only C has a similar pattern and is the correct answer.

2.

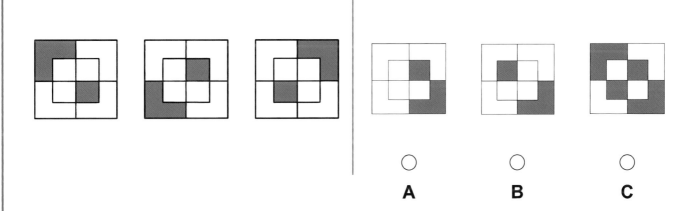

	A	B	C

B is correct. Your job is to find the option with the picture that most closely resembles the three pictures on the left. All the pictures on the left have a colored inner square opposite to a colored section of the outer square. Only B has a similar pattern and is the correct answer.

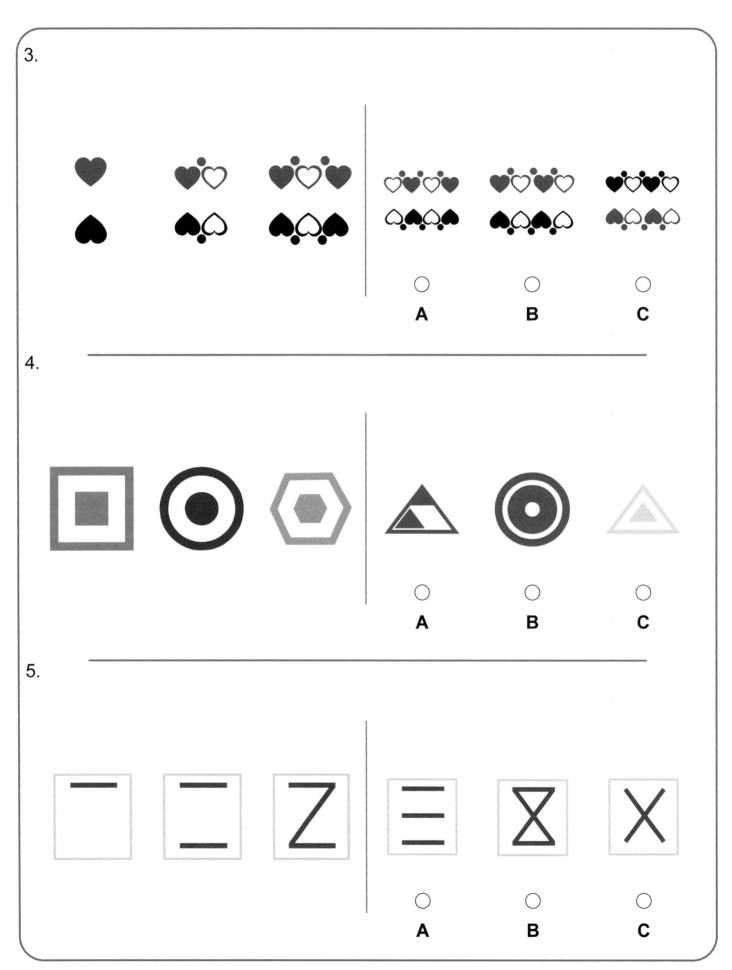

3.

4.

5.

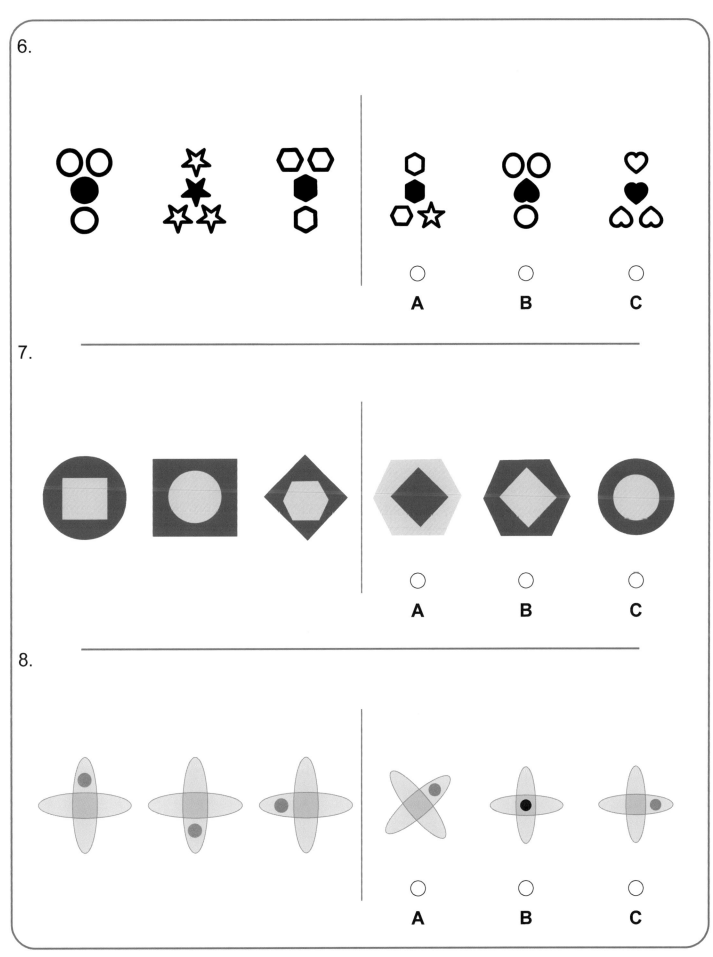

6.

7.

8.

9.

○   ○   ○
A   **B**   **C**

10.

○   ○   ○
A   **B**   **C**

11.

○   ○   ○
A   **B**   **C**

12.

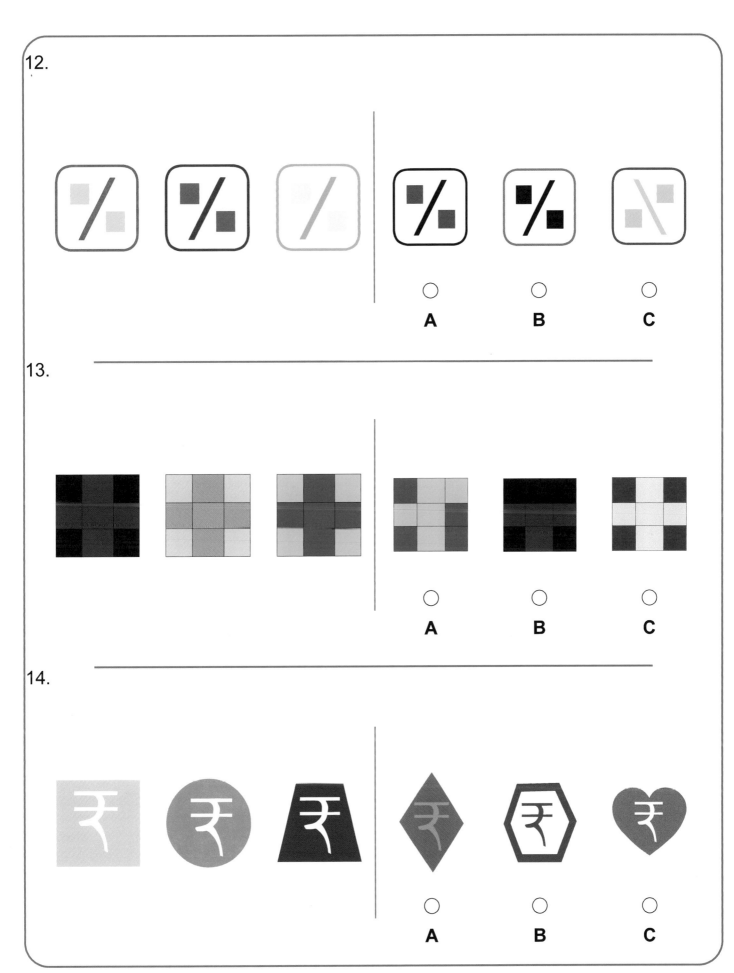

○ A   ○ B   ○ C

13.

○ A   ○ B   ○ C

14.

○ A   ○ B   ○ C

15.

○   ○   ○
A   **B**   **C**

16.

○   ○   ○
A   **B**   **C**

17.

○   ○   ○
A   **B**   **C**

18.

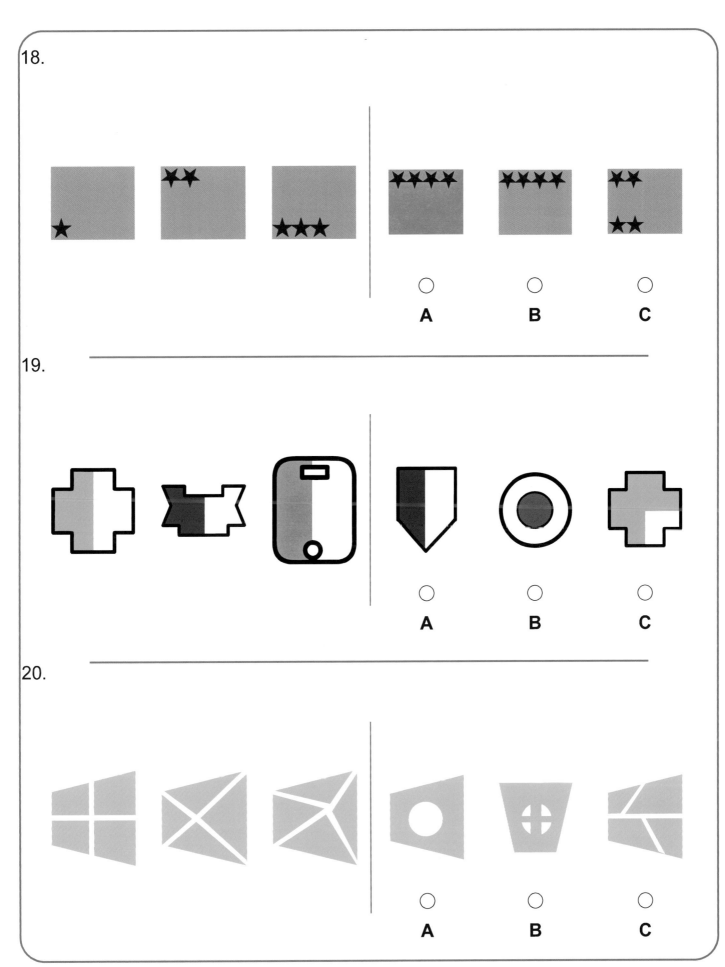

○   ○   ○
A   B   C

19.

○   ○   ○
A   B   C

20.

○   ○   ○
A   B   C

ANSWER KEY

Practice Test 1: All Subsets

Subset 1: Picture Analogies

Questions	1	2	3	4	5	6	7	8	9	10	11	12	13	14	15	16	17	18	19	20
Answers	C	A	C	B	A	A	C	C	B	C	A	B	A	B	B	A	A	C	C	C

Subset 2: Sentence Completion

Questions	1	2	3	4	5	6	7	8	9	10	11	12	13	14	15	16	17	18	19	
Answers	B	B	A	B	A	A	A	C	A	C	A	C	A	A	A	A	A	B	C	

Subset 3: Picture Classification

Questions	1	2	3	4	5	6	7	8	9	10	11	12	13	14	15	16	17	18	19	20
Answers	C	B	A	B	C	A	B	A	A	A	C	A	B	C	B	B	A	A	A	A

Subset 4: Number Analogies

Questions	1	2	3	4	5	6	7	8	9	10	11	12	13	14	15	16	17	18	19	20
Answers	C	B	A	C	A	C	A	C	A	B	A	C	A	C	B	C	B	B	A	A

Subset 5: Number Puzzles

Questions	1	2	3	4	5	6	7	8	9	10	11	12	13	14	15	16				
Answers	A	C	C	B	A	C	B	A	A	C	A	A	C	B	C	B				

Subset 6: Number Series

Questions	1	2	3	4	5	6	7	8	9	10	11	12	13	14	15	16	17	18	19	20
Answers	C	A	B	A	B	B	A	B	B	A	C	A	C	A	A	C	C	A	A	A

Subset 7: Figure Matrices

Questions	1	2	3	4	5	6	7	8	9	10	11	12	13	14	15	16	17	18	19	20
Answers	B	C	A	C	B	A	B	A	B	C	A	B	C	A	C	B	B	C	A	A

Subset 8: Paper Folding

Questions	1	2	3	4	5	6	7	8	9	10	11	12	13	14	15	16				
Answers	B	C	A	C	B	A	C	A	B	B	C	A	B	A	B	A				

Subset 9: Figure Classification

Questions	1	2	3	4	5	6	7	8	9	10	11	12	13	14	15	16	17	18	19	20
Answers	A	B	B	B	A	A	C	A	B	C	B	B	B	C	A	B	C	C	B	A

Answer Key

Practice Test 2: All Subsets

Subset 1: Picture Analogies

Questions	1	2	3	4	5	6	7	8	9	10	11	12	13	14	15	16	17	18	19	20
Answers	A	B	C	C	A	B	C	C	B	A	A	A	A	B	A	B	A	A	B	B

Subset 2: Sentence Completion

Questions	1	2	3	4	5	6	7	8	9	10	11	12	13	14	15	16	17	18	19	
Answers	C	C	B	B	A	A	B	C	A	B	A	B	C	A	B	B	C	B	A	

Subset 3: Picture Classification

Questions	1	2	3	4	5	6	7	8	9	10	11	12	13	14	15	16	17	18	19	20
Answers	B	C	C	C	C	C	C	B	A	B	A	B	A	A	B	A	A	C	A	B

Subset 4: Number Analogies

Questions	1	2	3	4	5	6	7	8	9	10	11	12	13	14	15	16	17	18	19	20
Answers	A	B	B	A	B	B	A	A	B	C	A	A	A	B	C	A	A	B	A

Subset 5: Number Puzzles

Questions	1	2	3	4	5	6	7	8	9	10	11	12	13	14	15	16				
Answers	A	C	B	A	A	A	A	C	C	C	B	C	B	A	B					

Subset 6: Number Series

Questions	1	2	3	4	5	6	7	8	9	10	11	12	13	14	15	16	17	18	19	20
Answers	B	C	B	A	C	B	A	A	B	A	B	A	C	A	B	B	A	C	B	A

Subset 7: Figure Matrices

Questions	1	2	3	4	5	6	7	8	9	10	11	12	13	14	15	16	17	18	19	20
Answers	B	B	A	C	A	A	B	B	C	C	A	A	C	A	C	B	C	A	B	A

Subset 8: Paper Folding

Questions	1	2	3	4	5	6	7	8	9	10	11	12	13	14	15	16				
Answers	B	C	A	C	A	A	C	A	C	C	B	B	B	B	C	C				

Subset 9: Figure Classification

Questions	1	2	3	4	5	6	7	8	9	10	11	12	13	14	15	16	17	18	19	20
Answers	C	B	B	C	B	C	B	C	B	A	C	A	C	C	A	A	C	B	A	C

Answer Key

Bonus – Your Free CogAT® Online Tutoring Lesson!*
(worth US$ 18.99)

Get your child a personal, one-on-one help on CogAT® from an expert at **www.Top-Grader.com.** Follow the below instructions to claim your free lesson:

1. Send your amazon order confirmation number or the copy of purchase invoice on email to <u>info@top-grader.com.</u>

2. A customer service representative will acknowledge the receipt of your mail and revert to you with a couple of options on the day and time for a 60 minute CogAT® lesson.

3. Select the day and time slot that works best for you and confirm it over the email.

4. You will receive a confirmation mail on your free lesson with set up details for the online class. You need a computer with internet connection to be able to take the online class.

5. A CogAT® expert will meet you and/or your child on the designated day and time to tutor him/her for 60 minutes.

*Terms and conditions apply. TOP GRADER LLC reserves the right to withdraw the bonus offer at any time without prior notice.

CPSIA information can be obtained at www.ICGtesting.com
Printed in the USA
LVIW01n1545071017
551594LV00017B/401